# MY WAY

A Unique and Personal Insight into the Changes in
Policing and Police Leadership Style Over the Years

## Kevin Moore

Published by Saron Publishers in 2018

The newspaper feature at Appendix A is reproduced by kind permission of Trinity Mirror and Paul Henderson

Cover montage is reproduced by kind permission of Mick Ewins bluelampprints.co.uk

The author's profits are being donated to the charity Care of Police Survivors (COPS), dedicated to helping the families of police officers who have losttheir lives on duty
www.ukcops.org

ISBN-13: 978-1-9999871-1-4


Saron Publishers
Pwllmeyrick House
Mamhilad
Mon
NP4 8RG

www.saronpublishers.co.uk

info@saronpublishers.co.uk

Follow us on Facebook and Twitter

# DEDICATION

This account is dedicated to all those colleagues I have worked with over almost forty years in policing, some of whom have become close friends in a way that only those who have worked within the Police Service can ever hope to understand.

Equally and arguably more importantly, it is also dedicated to my family and in particular my wonderful wife Ann, without whose unwavering support, my career in the police would not have been possible.

# ACKNOWLEDGEMENTS

I wish to begin by thanking my publisher, Penny Reeves of Saron Publishers, for her time, patience, sound professional advice and understanding in helping me to compile this book. This is especially the case taking into account that this is my first effort at putting together something of this nature.

Whilst *My Way* is about my policing career with a focus on the changes that have taken place over many years, clearly many of the influences on my career rely on many key individuals. This includes those who I have worked with, those that have worked for me and those that have helped to develop me.

Also, I wish to thank my many friends and colleagues for their unwavering support and friendship over the period of my long career. There are simply too many to list the names of here. However, you will all know who you are. Without you, what I have achieved over the years would not have been possible. Policing, perhaps more than any other profession in existence, relies on the men and women who serve within it for their dedication, team work, courage and public spiritedness. It has been my privilege to have worked with some of the very best in this regard.

However, I do specifically wish to acknowledge the influence of a number of individuals on my professional development over the years. These include; Jack Reece, Graham Hill, Chris Page, Jeremy Paine, Brian Foster, Mike Bennison, Roger Hills, Sir Ken Jones and Joe Edwards. Some of you, without perhaps even appreciating the fact, have been my mentors.

# Kevin Moore

I wish to acknowledge the part played by my father, John Moore, sadly deceased, on giving me some of the tools and early advice that were to prove so valuable later on in my working life. His common-sense approach to policing will remain in my memory for ever.

Lastly, but by no means least, I wish to acknowledge the contribution to my career and indeed my life by my wife Ann. Her support over the years has been incredible. Having been married very young and prior to me joining the police, she has experienced all the highs and lows and the pressures that a policing career brings with it. I owe her a tremendous debt of gratitude therefore.

# CONTENTS

# FOREWORD

The author spent almost forty years in policing, firstly as a police officer and then during the past more than eight years, operating as a member of police staff but still involved in the delivery of front line policing at a regional level, as part of the SE Regional Organised Crime Unit. Indeed, he is proud to say that his entire service was spent in an operational capacity.

As a police officer, he served for over thirty-one years within Sussex Police, the vast majority as a detective. He served at all ranks from detective constable through to and including detective chief superintendent as Head of Sussex CID. During those years, he led many homicide investigations and was acclaimed as a highly effective senior investigating officer. He also spent time as the divisional commander for the City of Brighton and Hove.

He has witnessed many changes to policing in his time. During his service, he gained a reputation for being an outspoken and no-nonsense leader with a determination to ensure that everything the police did was designed to enhance public safety by 'locking up the bad guys'. This included pushing the boundaries where appropriate and being 'lawfully audacious' whenever possible. Inevitably, during his service, he has attracted differing views on his leadership style and general approach to policing, both internally and externally, and many of these will be covered within the book. However, he would argue that he has always attempted to operate for the greater good of the public, never losing sight of the purpose of policing and the long-standing definition of a constable. In addition, he always tried to espouse the original principles of policing put in place by Sir Robert Peel, many of which have stood the test of time. In other words, he was determined to see that things were done in the right way or, as in the title of this book, *My Way*.

This book is a personal reflection on the changing face of policing and police leadership style over the past sixty years. Its purpose is to challenge the reader to achieve a greater understanding of how and why approaches have changed and how this has affected decision-making by operational leaders. It will hopefully provoke some thought as to what has influenced this, and whether this has been to the benefit or detriment of the police service.

The author has beeen able to draw on evidence spanning many years from the mid 1950s, when his father joined the police service, to the current day. As he enters full retirement, inevitably his thoughts have turned to the changing face of policing over this period and the drivers for this change, as well the culture underpinning this. Much of the account will contain a unique and personal insight based on the evidence gathered over a lifetime in policing, during which he achieved high rank and therefore mixed with some of the most senior leaders within the organisation. This has arguably given him a real opportunity to understand the mind-set of those working at the highest levels in policing. Many of his views may appear controversial but will be based on what he believes to be sound evidence- and are therefore honestly held. He will explore the thought processes that a senior police officer goes through in reaching key operational decisions and why, on occasions, these sometimes go wrong.

Finally, he will consider whether policing was better in the past than now, whether such perceptions are accurate and why these may have developed in the way that they have.

# CHAPTER 1 – IN THE BEGINNING

❖ Early memories of my father's police career and initial thoughts on discipline within the police service as well as respect and its basis - was this earned or learned?

❖ What influence did this have on me as an individual?

❖ The basis of local policing eg the village Bobby and connectivity with the public and the perception of respect between public and police. Was this real or imagined? Was there ever truly a 'Golden Age' of Policing? The perception of the autonomous local Bobby administering summary justice for minor misdemeanours.

❖ My decision to become a police officer and why?

My mum was busy vacuuming and dusting my father's office. She did this once a week as regular as clockwork. This time, however, she was paying even greater attention to doing a good job, because this day was the one each month when Sergeant Jim Thomas came to our house, inspected my father's office and checked his paperwork. Such was the policing regime at the time, almost militaristic in its methods, with discipline being uppermost.

At the beginning of the 1960s, my father was the village policeman at Broad Oak, Heathfield in East Sussex. His sergeant's regular visits were always something I and my younger sister and brother looked forward to, as Sergeant Thomas always gave us a sixpenny piece each, which bought a lot of sweets! My mother received an allowance from the police, to undertake the cleaning of the office which was adjacent to the police house in which we lived. In addition, she undertook such tasks as answering the phone when my father was out, as well as issuing 'movement of livestock licences' to the local farmers on occasions when my father was out working his beat. The set up in those days was very similar to scenes from the *Heartbeat* television series. Being given the responsibility of working a rural beat was seen by many as very prestigious and my father felt he was privileged to have gained such a posting so early in his service. It was, however, a 24/7 commitment and any phone calls or visits by the public to the house itself were expected, in the first instance at least, to be dealt with by my father, whether officially on or off duty. I wonder how many individuals would be keen to undertake such a role nowadays?!

However, it did have massive advantages as my father could operate as his own boss, so to speak, and the local bobby was one of the pillars of the community. It also meant that we were never without the odd turkey and vegetables at Christmas time, delivered to the doorstep anonymously by various local farmers! It made up for those occasions when the family was disturbed during the night by a caller to the house requiring assistance. This sometimes needed my father to go down the street to where he had parked his own car in order to transport a stranded member of the public who had missed the last bus or train from Heathfield and needed a lift. My father's only mode of transport for police purposes was a pedal cycle. Generally speaking, however, these were very happy days for us as a family and indeed the wider population. Village life operated at a much slower pace than wider society generally does in current times. Regardless of those who doubt what I am about to say, people seemed to be happier with their lot. Crime rates were relatively low and, much like the circumstances portrayed in *Heartbeat*, there was often the local rogue who was quickly identified as the perpetrator of a crime, similar to Claude Greengrass. Many incidents never made it to official recording stages, with a great number of minor matters dealt with through warnings and local redress. Sadly, as accountability has changed over the years, I doubt we will ever see those times again. At various stages, society appears to want a return to methods of less formal resolution but the reality is often different and we seem to delight in surrounding ourselves with copious amounts of bureaucracy.

My father and mother came from farming families, as indeed did many in the 1950s and 1960s. The industry thrived, particularly through the latter years, and there were many small farms run by tenant farmers. After my parents were married in the middle of the 1950s, they moved away to work on a farm in Oxfordshire, after a period when my father worked for one of our relatives on their farm. Around a year later, my father, who had been sent a copy of a local East Sussex newspaper, saw an advertisement requesting applications to join what was at that time known as the East Sussex Constabulary. In those days, what now constitutes Sussex Police was made up of East and West Sussex Constabularies as well as Hastings, Eastbourne and Brighton Borough forces. My father decided to apply, which was a big deal for him because his formal education had been fairly limited as he had rarely attended school from the age of thirteen as he worked on the farm. However, he must have made the best of the education that he did receive, as his ability with both the written word as well as arithmetic meant he passed the police entrance examination with flying colours. Indeed, I still have copies of his marks and he scored very highly. He was accepted into the service and in those days, was considered to be a relatively late joiner at the age of twenty-six. After completing his initial training at the former Sandgate Police Training Centre near Folkestone, a site that is now owned by Saga, he was posted to Hove. At this time, Hove was very much separate to Brighton and was still a part of the County of East Sussex.

# Kevin Moore

*My father's Passing Out Parade*

He had to take swimming lessons, as a pre-requisite of joining the force then was that individuals had to pass the bronze medallion life-saving qualification, because of the County's coastal nature. Failure to have achieved this would have meant my father's police career ending at an early stage, such were the times then. My parents lived in a rented flat in Glastonbury Road in Hove for which my father received a rent allowance as part of the terms and conditions of being a police officer. During their time there, I was born on 12th January 1957, actually in the old St Mary's Hospital in Eastbourne as my mother was staying with her parents. They had to wait a further few months before some new police houses in Stonecroft Close in Hove were completed. In comparison with what they were used to, this was luxury indeed.

My father continued to work as a police constable in Hove. I recall a story he told me regarding an occasion when he was due to report to a police box, away from Hove Police Station, to commence his early turn shift at 6am. When he arrived, he realised he had left the keys to the box at home. He had to cycle some two miles back home and then return in order to start his shift. He just about avoided being late for duty which was a disciplinary offence, and considered very serious for somebody still due to complete their two-year probationary period. He was sweating so much that, having booked on duty, he had to have a strip wash in the sink! In those days, officers wore their full uniform to and from work and this consisted of a heavy serge fabric which was exceedingly stiff and uncomfortable at the best of times. This was especially the case with the shirts, which had hard-wearing detachable collars. This was to assist individuals as it meant they only had to change their collars daily and their shirts every few days. Imagine that nowadays!

By a quirk of fate, my father was given the opportunity to take up the Broad Oak rural beat post which meant us moving back to the area where all our extended family still lived, most of whom were involved in farming in and around the area of Ashburnham and Brightling in East Sussex. Whilst still serving at Hove, my father, a keen and very useful footballer and cricketer, could still play for his previous local football team, Dallington. He was playing for them at Heathfield when, unfortunately, the changing rooms were broken into during the match and valuables belonging to some of the players, including my father, were stolen. The officer who attended was none other than Sergeant Jim Thomas. During the course of speaking to my father, he mentioned that the Broad Oak rural beat was due to become vacant and that, with his local roots, he should consider applying for it. Initially, Dad did not think he would have a chance of getting it as he was barely out of his probation but decided to apply anyway. Obviously, the rest is history, because he got the job and my parents, younger recently-born sister and I moved to Broad Oak. At the time, the village police officer was seen as a key figure in policing. Virtually every reasonably-sized village community across the whole country had its own 'Bobby'.

We spent over five happy years at Broad Oak, during which time my younger brother was born. Police pay was not great but living in a rent-free house, part of the terms and conditions, meant that my parents coped financially. I went to the local Broad Oak County Primary School, as did my sister, and we were very settled. My parents were involved in many local community events, such as flower and garden produce shows, jumble sales, whist drives, the parent/teachers association of the local school and many others. I believe that part of my understanding of the police culture was probably developed in me from a relatively early age. This was because, more so in those days than more recent times, social activities for police officers and their families were often linked to the police organisation. There were Christmas parties and pantomimes for the children of police officers to attend. Also, there were trips to the zoo and similar activities arranged through the local police social club. We always seemed to be involved in something that was going on.

Police officers were moved around fairly regularly and five years in any post was pretty much the limit. The fact that practically all officers lived in police accommodation helped with this flexibility, because the costs incurred by the police service only involved a removal lorry and some resettlement allowances. Therefore, when my Dad's time was up, we found ourselves being moved to a different rural beat officer's posting at Winchelsea, near Rye. This took place at the beginning of 1965 when I had just passed my eighth birthday. It was very similar to what we were used to. However, during our early days there, my mother found it difficult to settle and my father was starting to think about what he might wish to move on to, in terms of his police career. He was keen to become a traffic officer and was in the process of completing his attachment to that department, as well as attending advanced driver training courses at Maidstone in Kent. Around this time, police officers were just starting to take advantage of the rent allowance they could receive in lieu of a police house, in order to purchase their own homes. This was a major step forward and one which had a considerable impact on policing. It meant officers could not be moved around with the freedom that had once existed, because the Police Authority were responsible for costs related to the buying and selling of their homes, if the move was far enough away. By the late 1980s, police authorities started to sell off elements of the police estate, including police houses, to the extent where by the early 1990s, there were few, if any, police houses left. Arguably, this could be seen as a little like selling the family silver as they would never be able to reverse such a decision. This of course became more of an issue with rising house prices later on which meant that many young police officers could not afford to buy their own homes. In hindsight therefore, the availability of police houses may have helped. However, at the time, the cost of maintaining these was deemed excessive.

My parents, having mustered a deposit, decided to buy their first home in the village of Peasmarsh, near Rye. As a result, after less than a year, the family left Winchelsea behind and started on a new adventure. I attended the local Peasmarsh Primary School, along with my sister and brother. Around this time, Dad joined the local traffic division and very quickly moved to riding a police motorcycle, a Norton Commando. He could often bring his bike home which meant I was the envy of my school friends who all had to come and inspect the bike when it was on our

# Kevin Moore

*My father's prized police motorcycle*

driveway. Later on, my father, who had passed his sergeant's examination, was successful in achieving promotion. Fortunately, for us as a family, he was posted to Rye which meant there was no further upheaval in terms of us having to move. By now, I was well through my secondary education, attending the Thomas Peacocke Comprehensive School in Rye. I can honestly say that, whilst I had the utmost respect for what my Dad did in terms of his career, I did not at this stage hold any aspiration to become a police officer myself. Indeed, because of my sporting prowess, I was looking to become a PE Teacher, having represented the County at both football and cricket. At no time in my formative years did I receive any adverse attention from school friends or elsewhere regarding my father's chosen occupation, other than some minor leg pulling. Indeed, Sergeant Moore was well-known and respected, not only within our local village but also within the Rye area, for being firm but fair, as well as for his common-sense approach to the use of discretion. He was also well-known for being able to handle himself physically, as shown one night in Rye when some young troublemakers from Kent decided to 'do battle' with some of the locals. What took place became known as the Battle of Conduit Hill. My father and his colleagues won the day and the local magistrates dispensed justice appropriately. However, my street cred went up considerably due to my father's involvement! The respect my father enjoyed came from young and old, and he had a wide circle of friends and acquaintances outside the police service. I feel that the vast majority of the population at this time respected, even if they did not necessarily like, the police and I believe this continued for many more years, including most of my own police service. Was there ever such a thing as a 'Golden Age' of policing? I am not sure that there was as such.

This issue is worth further consideration at this point because I have always felt there are in existence a number of myths that still abound to this day as to what went on within policing and the relationship between police and public. The most obvious is the infamous 'clip round the ear', administered to local miscreants guilty of minor offending such as 'scrumping' apples. I grew up in villages during most of my early life and I never saw such activity, despite having been involved with others in the commission of minor misdemeanours which came to the attention of the local Peasmarsh bobby, PC Ron Peters! There have been many authors from the academic world, writing on police-related matters, who have stated that the whole issue of the 'Golden Age' of policing is itself a figment of the public's imagination. They believe such views are similar to those held by people who honestly believe that summers past were all warm and sunny! Many academics are of the opinion that the majority of the public, and in particular the working classes, resented the imposition of policing upon them, believing the organisation to be an arm of the state, put in place to control them. Regardless of this, in the past most people respected and even liked the police, as proved through public attitude surveys conducted over periods of years. This comes to the fore, particularly when a police officer tragically loses their life whilst on duty. It is also noticeable how, at one time, not so many years ago, the police as an institution were amongst those held in the highest regard in terms of the levels of trust held in them by members of the public. In more recent times those numbers have fallen away. This is something I will consider again later on within this book.

As I continued to grow up, I saw at first hand, through my father, some of the developments in policing. What was apparent was the presence of strict management structures and the adherence to a very disciplined regime. The organisation was clearly rank-conscious and there was an easily identifiable hierarchical structure in place. What struck me in the talks I had with my father was that those within the police service identified readily with this and were happy to work within that structure. There was a clarity of purpose and everyone seemed to know their position within the laid-down order of things. Dad had a small team for whom he had responsibility and they came to him to authorise decisions that required his involvement. He in turn was answerable to the local inspector and chief inspector and I would regularly hear him in telephone conversations with them at home. It was clear he had a relationship with them similar to the one his team members had with him. Unsurprising then that the police, in those times, recruited large numbers of people from the military. This was the case up until and indeed after I joined the service at the end of the 1970s.

# MY WAY

Many people make the mistake of believing that a place like Rye represents a quiet backwater. However, two particular cases made national news headlines. One, at the beginning of the 1970s, involved a local fisherman bringing a large number of illegal immigrants into the country at Jury's Gap near Camber Sands. The plot, involving several Pakistanis being brought across from the continent, was foiled through the efforts of HM Coastguard and HM Customs, and the offender received a sentence of several years' imprisonment. This case was highly unusual at the time, before such events involving what is now known as human trafficking became as newsworthy as they are today.

The second involved the kidnap of Lady Devonport from her manor house in Peasmarsh by a local man, later convicted of the crime. I recall some of the details of this case as my father was on duty when it happened. The offender, a man named Peter Mathews, was a member of a local farming family. He was well known in the Rye area and was a very good cricketer, playing for the town for many years. He got heavily into debt and therefore decided, somewhat bizarrely, many would suggest, to kidnap the Viscountess Lady Devonport. She lived in the family home known as Peasmarsh Place, and during the early hours one morning, Mathews managed to gain access to the building. He forcibly took hold of her ladyship and dragged her across field a few miles to where he lived in a village called Playden which is near Rye.

He kept her tied up in an outbuilding in what was the middle of winter and therefore she was at risk of becoming hypothermic. Indeed, she was a very elderly woman, obviously made of strong stuff because she managed to survive her ordeal. A police dog tracked the route taken by Mathews and fortunately, Lady Devonport was thus found fairly quickly. He was later tried at The Old Bailey and received a substantial prison sentence. The officer in the case was Jack Reece who later became Head of the CID in Sussex and led the Grand Hotel bombing case in Brighton in 1984.

As I approached my A Level examinations, I was struggling to decide what I wanted to do when I left the sixth form. In those days, only elite pupils went on to university and I was certainly not a member of that particular group. I had been for a couple of interviews to teacher training colleges and these had helped me decide that my future did not belong in teaching. Needless to say, my parents were keen for me to decide quickly what it was that I wanted to do, as time was getting on. My father had a PC working for him who had previously worked in a bank. It was a steady enough job with, it appeared, some prospects, and lacking any better ideas, I applied to Barclays Bank and the Trustee Savings Bank. I had interviews with both and each accepted me, pending future vacancies. The TSB contacted me first and so in 1975, I began my banking career at their local Hastings Branch.

Things were going okay and whilst working, I started day release at the local College of Further Education in order to undertake studies for an ONC in Business Studies, which had taken the place of the more traditional Banking Examinations. During these early days, I met the woman who was soon to become my wife, Ann. Despite both of us being relatively young, we became engaged fairly quickly and were married in August 1977. By now, I had passed the first year of my two-year course but there were no guarantees of promotion in the bank, even with the ONC under my belt. I had responsibilities now and my bank salary was not great. I started to think about the future and I suppose it was somewhat inevitable that I seriously began to think a career in the police would be a good move. My father had never done anything to encourage such a move but when I told him I had decided to apply in early 1978, he was very supportive. I had decided I was not really either happy or fulfilled, working in the banking world. It was all too methodical and mundane, to be honest, and I felt I needed something more challenging and stimulating. I had always deep down possessed a strong service ethic and I felt that, as a police officer, I could achieve both of those aims. Of course, I had also had the benefit of witnessing at first-hand what a great job it was, through my dad's involvement. At the time, police salaries were not considered great and many were leaving, leading to the Labour Government commissioning a report from Lord Edmund Davies in 1978. This took a fresh look at police salaries and conditions generally which led to their considerable improvement over the next few years. Up until this point in time, it was not unusual for police officers to have little 'side lines'. Some had particular trade skills and at Rye, there was an electrician, a baker, a sign writer and a builder. Others, including my own father, used to undertake gardening, hop picking and other labouring-type work. I remember in the summer of 1965 when we were at Winchelsea, my dad, together with a local man, earned extra money by digging out and concreting caravan bases at one of the holiday parks located at Winchelsea Beach. I was eight years old and used to help and get paid in Coke and crisps!

At the time of my application, police service terms and conditions were still better than what I was receiving in the bank, especially when free accommodation or a rent allowance was part of the overall package. I submitted my application and was interviewed at Sussex Police Headquarters at Lewes on 26th May 1978. I didn't have to take the entrance examination as I had the minimum five O Levels including Maths and English. My interview was chaired by a chief superintendent, accompanied by another chief superintendent and a superintendent, all in full uniform. I remember being somewhat in awe in the presence of such senior police officers but I quickly settled my nerves and gave a pretty good account of myself, including my reasons for wanting to join the police. I was accepted that day following a medical and I rushed back to my bank in Hastings to hand in my notice that afternoon, in order to take up the offer of a place in the next intake of 26th June. I remember being terribly excited and proud. From a phone box, I phoned Ann at work to let her know and then, of course, my father who was delighted. So, it was decided. I was to join Sussex Police. I could never in my wildest dreams have ever imagined what I was to subsequently experience in terms of a career in policing.

# CHAPTER 2 – THE EARLY DAYS

- ❖ Initial police training – early discipline and its impact.
- ❖ Initial impressions of police leadership styles – hierarchical, militaristic influence, rank structure.
- ❖ Early influences and organisational culture.
- ❖ Police leadership at that time - Was it oppressive or clear and direct leadership?
- ❖ Respect – what was its basis?
- ❖ The public and the police – perceptions and relationships.
- ❖ Policing Brighton in the late 1970s. What it was like then and the difference.
- ❖ The 'Police Family' – what it was then and what it has become now.
- ❖ Influences on Policing – The Brixton Riots 1981 and the Scarman Report; The Broadwater Farm Riots.

Early on the morning of Monday 26th June 1978, one of Sussex Police's newest recruits set off from his home in St Leonards, having kissed his young wife goodbye. Ann and I couldn't afford a car so, suitcase in hand, I was making the short walk to Warrior Square, St Leonards railway station, to catch the train to Lewes. Indeed, we lived very modestly at that time in a second floor rented flat on the seafront in St Leonards.

I felt somewhat apprehensive and nervous on the journey to attend a week of induction training at Lewes Headquarters. This preceded a ten-week police training course at Ashford Police Training Centre, followed by a further week back at Lewes, undertaking what was known as the local procedure course. Following this, we would then go to our divisions, having learned our fate as regards our postings in week seven at Ashford. I guess most of my concern related to what seemed to be a massive step into the unknown, despite my father being a policeman of well over twenty years' standing. Even taking this into account, I was still concerned as to how I would cope with a career in policing. I was also conscious that this was it now. I had burned my bridges with the TSB and was embarking on what would hopefully be a thirty-year career, as long as I successfully completed my initial two-year probationary period. The twelve weeks of training was residential and I was also concerned that, having been married for less than a year, I was leaving Ann on her own. We had no telephone and therefore for me, letters were the main form of communication. Imagine facing a world like that today, bearing in mind our reliance on the social media network!

In more recent times, initial residential training has ceased. One reason for this was that it was felt in some quarters that such a level of commitment may have discriminated against some individuals and in particular, women who were mothers. I personally think this was a shame as I feel the experience was character-building, and set a tone in terms of self-discipline. Various models have since been trialled. One involved the initial training being undertaken through Universities and potentially used as a first step towards a degree. This academic element  ran alongside Probationer Development Units or PDUs, based on police divisions, where newly-recruited officers worked alongside experienced PCs known as tutor constables. The approach was far more structured and was similar to that adopted in other professions, involving a modular system. Since 2010, things have altered again in the face of funding cuts which led to very limited, or indeed in some places, no recruitment. Less focus has been placed on the University element and more emphasis directed towards self-development. This means that police officer recruits need to have demonstrated their future commitment through having worked as a PCSO or Special Constable for a period of time. In a similar vein, there is an expectation that recruits will have undertaken a degree in their own time and at their own expense. Things are therefore considerably different, especially when coupled with the advent of direct recruitment to Inspector and Superintendent levels.

I still recall vividly my very first day as a police officer. Having arrived at Lewes HQ, met the other new recruits and made our formal introductions, we were off to Lewes Magistrates Court to be sworn in as police officers. I remember how proud I felt as I swore my oath of allegiance to the Queen. I understood, even at this stage, that a police officer was uniquely different to any other employee in that we were in fact servants of the Crown.

It is worth recalling the wording of the oath:

*I, Kevin John Moore, do solemnly and sincerely declare and affirm that I will truly serve our Sovereign Lady the Queen in the office of Constable, without favour or affection, malice or ill will; and that I will, to the best of my power, cause the peace to be kept and preserved and prevent all offences against the persons and properties of Her Majesty's subjects and that while I continue to hold the said office I will, to the best of my skill and knowledge, discharge all the duties thereof faithfully according to the law.*

Looking back, I really believe that, whether consciously or subconsciously, I carried out my duties with this at the forefront of my mind from that day onwards.

Another day was spent being fitted, in the loosest sense of the term, with our uniforms. This was my first experience of dealing with Dennis Myatt, a retired police officer, now manager of the uniform clothing stores. He issued items of uniform as if the money to pay for them came from his own pocket! We each had to sign for all items of uniform and equipment we received, and woe betide anyone who lost or damaged anything. The rest of the week was spent carrying out various exercises and receiving inputs from the training sergeants and the inspector, on what to expect in our initial training, as well as general points regarding police work. Everything was so disciplined. We addressed the sergeants in terms of rank and surname, and when the inspector entered the room, we stood up behind our desks. However, it provided a real insight into what we could expect at the District Training Centre at Ashford which we would be attending the following Sunday afternoon. We finished slightly early on the Friday which gave me time to purchase a pair of parade boots and Doctor Marten shoes. I was somewhat surprised to hear we would be undertaking drill at the training centre, thus reinforcing the somewhat militaristic approach to things in the police service at the time. I also had to have my hair cut as, despite it being relatively short already, I had been told was too long.

Sunday arrived, and I was off on the train again to Ashford. When I arrived at the PTC, it was to discover there were other trainee officers from Kent, Surrey, Hampshire and British Transport Police as well as Sussex. We were told which of the five classes we were in and shown to our rooms, our home for the next ten weeks. There were four officers to a room, with the female officers having their own residential block. This of course meant that individuals had to quickly acclimatise to the habits of the others sharing the room, such as snoring and farting! I was also somewhat perturbed to find that each class had to perform a 'duty weekend' at the centre. Having been allocated to A Class, mine would be the following weekend. So I had to work out how to get a letter to Ann as soon as possible, to tell her I would not see her for two weeks. Just as well she is made of stern stuff.

*A Class at Ashford District Training Centre*

Training Centre life was very regimented and structured. We got up around 6.30am, shaved and showered, had breakfast, about the only edible meal of the day, and then attended parade and inspection, before going to classes to learn the law. The only exception was the morning we went into Ashford to the local swimming pool for life saving training. Minor disciplinary breaches meant having to attend the dreaded 9pm parade where individuals had to parade in full dress uniform for inspection by the duty sergeant. I made it my aim to avoid this indignity and thankfully managed to achieve this. In order to emphasise the military nature of things, all trainees had to wear their helmets outdoors and if we passed an officer of inspector rank or above, we had to salute that individual. Every Monday there was an examination with an 80% pass mark, and failure to achieve this meant attendance at remedial sessions in the evenings in order to resit and pass that particular exam. Three failures meant being asked to leave.

These were supplemented by an intermediate and final examination which had to be passed to a similar standard. Luckily I excelled at these and was the second-highest marked student for the whole intake, just missing out to a university graduate who was awarded the Baton of Honour.

There were also inter-class sports competitions involving cricket, basketball and volleyball. Due to my sporting background, I competed in each event and A Class won all three. Things were highly competitive, both in terms of the various classes as well the sergeants for each class. There were two allocated for every class and I remember mine to this day - Graham Wyeth from Hampshire who went on to become a temporary Assistant Chief Constable, and Malcolm Rouse from Kent who retired as an inspector. They were excellent and possessed an infectious energy and enthusiasm. We only had two students fail one exam each in the whole ten weeks, which is a tribute to their teaching methods.

Other elements of training involved the dreaded practical tests where the training sergeants acted out the parts of offenders in relation to elements of the law that we had been taught. The selected trainees would then be appointed to deal with the incident as they saw things, as if it were a real-life situation. These practical tests were seen as a bit of a no-win situation. This was because if it was going too well for you, one of the sergeants would invariably *ad lib* and throw a spanner in the works, in order to ensure that you didn't get too complacent or cocky. Finally, there was the constant bulling of boots and pressing of uniforms, in order to pass the inspections held throughout the course. On the first morning, despite my recent haircut, I was told, along with many others, to report to the onsite barber. That haircut was so short, it actually lasted me for the whole of the ten weeks!

Week seven arrived and we were all keen to find out where we would be posted after training. I had lived all my life in East Sussex and I was hoping for a posting to either Hastings or Eastbourne. However, it was not to be. I was given Brighton. I had hardly ever been to the place, let alone lived there. Ann had hardly been much further east than Hastings and here we were off to Brighton. However, we quickly got used to the idea and, from a policing perspective, it was the best thing that could ever have happened, as I learned so much there.

At the end of the ten weeks at Ashford, we had a passing out parade which Ann, my parents and Ann's mother and father all attended. The night before, there was a dining-in night which was probably the only time a decent meal was served! As I was married, Ann was allowed to attend and I was permitted to spend the night in a hotel with her. A major thing indeed! Speaking of the food at Ashford, although I was as fit as a fiddle and at almost six feet and two inches, was only 12 and a half stone, I still managed to lose half a stone during the ten-week course!

Having completed initial training, it was back to Lewes HQ for a week's local procedure course. This was spent looking at the local forms and paperwork requirements as well as dealing generally with issues unique to Sussex and thus not covered at Ashford. By now, I just wanted to get to Brighton. Ann and I had moved into our police-owned flat in the Hollingdean area of the town and were reasonably well settled in. She had found herself a new job and I was impatient to get started in 'the job'.

My first day at Brighton was very much an introductory one. In the afternoon, I went out to crew the town centre area car which was great. I started to get a feel for the real thing and I couldn't wait to join my section which happened the following day on an early turn shift. This involved 6am starts with a 2pm finish. The shift pattern in those days, and pretty much everywhere across the country, was late, night and early shifts ie week and week about, 2pm to 10pm then 6am to 2pm and finally 10pm to 6am, with days off in between. Early turn started on a Friday and so I was down to complete Tuesday, Wednesday and Thursday early turns. On my first duty, I met my colleagues, including my first sergeant Colin Ridley and the shift inspector Joe White. The shifts in those days were around twenty-five, massive compared to nowadays. Interestingly, there was only one female constable on the section, a reflection of the imbalance of male to female officers which prevailed at this time. It started to change very soon afterwards as more female officers were recruited. The reason for these low numbers was because female officers had only fairly recently started working alongside their male colleagues. Previously, there had been specialist policewomen's departments.

Getting to know everyone was quite a task. I was part of C Section, or C Column on C2. Brighton itself was split into two. C1 broadly covered to the west side of the Palace Pier and upwards to include Patcham, up to the boundary with Hove, with C2 covering everything to the east stretching to Telscombe Cliffs. In these early days, I was very aware I was the junior member of the section and therefore saw my peers as individuals to look up to as well as learn from. I only had a tutor constable for a very few shifts before being told I would be working on my own. This was quite unusual, even in those days, but majorly different from recent times. Some would argue that new police officers should be encouraged to stand on their own feet sooner than they do nowadays.

I quickly settled into the routine and was really enjoying my new job. At that time, officers were encouraged to be very proactive when working their beats. You needed to know who, in terms of known criminals, lived where, what vehicles they owned and who they mixed with. The Collator's office at Brighton was a must visit place as he was a mine of information and would often task officers to gain what is now referred to as intelligence, in order to update records. We were also expected to stop individuals and vehicles and conduct checks, particularly late at night and in the early hours of the morning. There was a need to show an ability to undertake self-generated arrests of suspects, rather than just respond to matters to which officers were sent. Once allocated a beat, there were always large numbers of enquiries that had to be undertaken. These included the service on individuals of a summons to appear at court, the execution of arrest warrants, as well as interviewing subjects believed to have been involved in motoring offences committed in other police areas. This was a great way of getting to know your beat and who lived there and how known criminals operated within it. I was getting very positive feedback from my sergeant and my peers and I was also still doing well on the probationer officer courses held at Lewes HQ where my marks were among the highest. Sadly, around the end of October, personal tragedy struck.

I was walking my beat along Queen's Park Road on a Thursday late turn shift. It was 2nd November 1978. I received a call on my police radio to return to the station to see my inspector. You can imagine my first thought was that I must have done something wrong. A short while later, I sat in Inspector Joe White's office to be told my father had been rushed to St Helen's Hospital in Hastings. He was described as being seriously ill. I knew he had not been well for some months, apparently suffering from anaemia, and he had taken periods of sick leave. However, when I had spoken to my mother periodically on the phone, she did not appear unduly concerned. In short, my father was very belatedly diagnosed as suffering from leukaemia. He was only forty-eight years of age and still serving as a police officer. Although he was admitted to the specialist Hammersmith Hospital in London, he was so ill that, despite undergoing chemotherapy treatment, he caught an infection and died on 9th December. The police funeral for Dad was just incredibly emotional and is an event I will never forget. To see the guard of honour provided by officers of the Traffic Division will live in my memory for ever. The support my family and I received in the weeks and months to follow was second to none. I was so proud to be a member of an organisation that made such an effort to look after its own. It was at this point that I realised the true meaning of 'the police family'. Today, it is used to describe the joint elements of policing including special constables, PCSOs (Police Community Support Officers), volunteers and some members of other law enforcement agencies. I have always believed it describes a camaraderie and relationship between members of the organisation that is as close as anything can be. This was the police service that I joined and the one that existed for many years afterwards. The effects upon me personally really did not show for several months, until it finally registered that I would never again see my father. At the age of twenty-one years, I was really at a point where I truly appreciated my father's company and he left a massive gap in my life. To some extent, even to this very day, I have regretted the fact I have never been in a position to share my achievements within the police service with him.

Whilst the impact of Dad's death inevitably impacted on me for months to come, it also served to drive me on in terms of my police career. I became even more determined to make a success of life as a police officer, not only to fulfil my own wishes but also to make him proud of me, although, at this particular time, I had no real aspiration to achieve promotion. I was still performing well 'on the streets' and unusually for someone so young in service, my inspector put me forward for a light-weight motorcycle course, followed shortly afterwards by a standard police car driving course. Probationer constables rarely saw the inside of a police car in those days and therefore this was some measure in my own mind as to how well I was progressing. This also meant that I could access the best duties where things were busiest.

I was privileged to work on a section with some really good police officers, a number of whom were what are known as real 'thief takers' ie individuals who had a real copper's nose for identifying proactively those individuals guilty of committing crime. One good example involved a PC named 'Jock' Edgar. I worked with him on a number of occasions where he would suggest stopping a particular individual who was walking or a car that was being driven. It would often be the case that the individual was in possession of stolen property from a burglary or the car being driven was a recently stolen one as yet not reported to the police. His hit rate for such success was quite incredible! I learned so much from them all and this undoubtedly held me in good stead for the future. I will be forever grateful to them.

Some senior police officers today believe and indeed like to portray an image that 'neighbourhood policing', as it is titled today, is a new thing. This is definitely not the case and a version of it has existed in policing since it first started. As beat officers, we relied very greatly on the receipt of information from the public and other sources, hence the need to get to know those living on your 'manor'. In the days when I was working a motorcycle beat which took in the east of Brighton, I received information, which I passed to CID, from a resident whom I had let off with an informal caution for having a bald tyre on his car. This in turn led to the arrest and conviction of several suspects for a series of burglaries committed on an industrial estate in Woodingdean.

Policing in Brighton in those days was far different from now, undertaken with an 'iron fist' rather than a 'velvet glove'. The police were on top of things most of the time and the public in the main respected us for it. There was a real no nonsense approach, and criminal or other bad behaviour was simply not tolerated and was stamped on hard. Today, there is a lot more accountability and therefore much of what went on 'unofficially' historically would probably not be accepted today. However, my own experience, having spoken to many non-police law-abiding friends from a broad cross section of society, is that they expect and want to witness strong policing. Sadly, over the years, I believe that a small majority have been listened to too readily, leading to the development of a police service that is now often afraid to operate with a physical show of strength.

Bank Holidays in Brighton often meant trouble. The end of the 1970s and beginning of the 1980s saw a reincarnation of the Mods and Rockers era, as well as large groups of other trouble makers, hell bent on causing trouble and disrupting the peace and tranquillity which most visitors to Brighton wanted. These individuals received pretty short shrift from the local police. We were given long shifts and there was a no-nonsense approach by officers on mobile units, which consisted of a Landrover containing a sergeant and six constables. This message was passed on loud and clear by senior officers at the morning briefings. Many of these were certainly not afraid to roll up their sleeves and join the front line in dealing with problems! Often, incidents that officers were sent to involved fights between different factions. These were usually resolved through the use of reasonable force summary justice! In those days, no one on the other end of this tended to complain and such actions were accepted by offenders and public alike. The public expected the police to 'sort things out'. To demonstrate how things worked then, I recall one occasion, where a couple of hundred trouble makers had their shoe laces tied together, before being marched to the railway station and put on a special train, commissioned to take them all back to

London. As I said previously, you would never get away with such action now! There would be individuals or groups somewhere who would succeed in gaining media attention to sound off about breaches of human rights etc.

There were some real characters in the police service in those times and we had a number of these in Brighton. I remember in particular our Station Sergeant John McCann. He was having difficulty one day with an individual in the front office area whom I thought I recognised. During a break in proceedings, I asked John who the man was. When he told me, I remembered the name and told John I had a non-payment of fine warrant for the man, held in the police box in Woodingdean. He told me to fetch it. On my return, he asked me if the warrant was backed for bail. On checking, I noted that it was and told him so. He told me to give him the warrant and he duly drew two lines across the bail section and said words to the effect that it was no longer backed for bail and told me to arrest him. The man was kept in custody until court in the morning. John just looked at me and winked saying, 'That will teach him!'

In a similar vein, I recall working a mobile unit with a sergeant called Bob Dipper, a tough rugby player and as hard as nails. We were sent to deal with a major disturbance at one of the night clubs. On arrival and from the street, the scene looked like something from a bar in the Wild West. There were people lying on the floor covered in blood and injured, and we PCs made to get out of the Landrover quickly to deal with the situation. Bob told us to sit tight and allow things to calm down a bit. After a few minutes, we entered the premises. Things had calmed down considerably by now and we made a few arrests, tidied up and returned to the police station in a totally calm manner. A highly common-sense approach to a volatile situation!

To further demonstrate that things were not always dealt

with by the book, I recall an occasion when I was crewed, together with another officer, more experienced than I, in the town centre car. We were sent to deal with a drunken individual in Madeira Drive. My colleague was reluctant to tie us up with dealing with a drunk and promptly put him in the back of the car. We then drove to Sheepcote Valley on the outskirts of the town where the drunken man was removed from the car and left to his own devices. Job done, we thought. However, a short while later, we received a call to attend a telephone box at Sheepcote Valley to speak to a man who claimed he had been kidnapped by police officers and dumped at Sheepcote Valley! Happy days!

There was also a 'zero tolerance' approach to matters involving homosexual acts in public toilets. Whilst the Sexual Offences Act of 1967 had legalised homosexual acts committed in private between consenting male adults, any such acts committed in a public place still, to this day, constitute a criminal offence and were policed rigorously then. At the time, a Vice Squad was a permanent feature of policing in Brighton. Officers, normally from the uniform branch, were seconded to the squad for up to six-monthly periods. Whilst Brighton was known for its somewhat seedy side which included prostitution and other somewhat devious behaviour dating back over many years, the Vice Squad did seem to major on illegal homosexual activity. The fact that many called this Unit the 'Bog Squad' probably gives some idea as to how the officers spent a large proportion of their time. Even then, I thought there seemed to be something fairly unpalatable about having a couple of police officers in a loft space in public toilets, trying to catch those in the commission of illegal sex acts. Whilst such matters were illegal then and are still illegal to this day, I am sure that in the current climate, even if police resources allowed, such tactics would face severe criticism. This style of policing is unlikely to be tolerated nowadays in a city that is perceived to be one of the LGBT capitals of the country, if not the world. Any such action would, I am sure, lead to the police being accused of homophobia.

During an officer's probationary period, individuals carried out two separate fortnightly attachments to the CID and the Traffic Department. The aim was to heighten knowledge on the part of those officers, as well as giving them an insight into the activities of those teams. It needs to be remembered that, then, there were broadly three main elements to policing ie Uniform Patrol, CID and Traffic Policing. Whilst there were other small specialist units such as Scenes of Crime, the Mounted Section and Dog Section, there were certainly not the plethora of specialisms that exist today. I will focus on the merits and dis-benefits of this at a later stage. Suffice it to say that the numbers required for these can only come from one place and that is the Uniform Patrol area. As I touched on previously, at the time that I joined, we could parade around twenty-five officers on any given shift. Nowadays, it's a tiny proportion of that number who take to the streets at any one time. To emphasise this, I recall attending a public meeting many years later whilst I was the Divisional Commander for Brighton and Hove and asking those attending how many uniformed officers they thought were deployed on an average night shift. The numbers suggested varied but it would be fair to say that those people were flabbergasted as to how few there were in reality. In terms of my attachments to Traffic and CID, I have to say that, while I did enjoy my time spent with Traffic and those I worked with made me feel very welcome, I also had a great time with the CID, and I believe it was this that formed my thinking as to where I might want to focus my future career aspirations. While it was genuinely a little like the fictional *Life on Mars* television series, there really were some excellent detectives around. I learned so much from those I worked with in the short time I had with them, and it really whetted my appetite for more. However, in the interim, I was to move in a somewhat different direction.

During my probationary period at Brighton, I was also representing the division and the Force at football, and played cricket on occasions for the Force also. I was lucky that my inspector Joe White recognised the value of having one of his team represent his section in this way. While Force level sport was supported through allowing participation in duty time, and divisional sport was half and half, it still required a high degree of give and take on all sides.

Having completed my local probationer training, which consisted of five, week-long courses at Lewes HQ, I was off to Ashford PTC to undertake the final part of my initial training, known as the Continuation Course which was of two weeks' duration. We had officers from other forces with us again on this occasion, including some from outside the traditional SE Region. Some colleagues from my initial ten-week training course, however, were also in attendance. It was an excellent two weeks and of course at the time, there were two ten-week training courses ongoing for new recruits. This meant that we were the senior constables and the reins were loosened just a little, in terms of the more disciplined elements! However, the food was just as bad! We did have to take exams again and this time, I achieved the highest marks overall. While my academic achievements at school were ordinary to say the least, I seemed to excel in the learning of the law and its application. This assisted me greatly later when I performed well in my promotion examinations. A short few months after completing the Continuation Course, officers were given the news as to whether they would be 'signed off' as having successfully completed their probation. This was usually a formality, because, in those days, individuals who were not viewed as being likely to make the grade were generally rooted out well before this time! Things were fairly harsh in this respect and I witnessed at first hand several individuals who were pressured into resigning. It was important that not only did an individual need to impress their sergeant and inspector, but also the senior constables on the section. I learned a lot in my first two years at Brighton and I have reason to be grateful to many of the officers who looked after me. There was a real team spirit in existence. At the end of the early turn week, the whole section would go up to the bar in the evening. Wives, husbands, girlfriends and boyfriends also attended, prior to the start of our long weekend off duty, consisting of the Friday, Saturday and Sunday. In reality, we used to often work at least one of those days for overtime. The social aspect to those occasions and its benefits could not be underestimated, however. It was pretty much a three-line whip to attend and only those away on holiday or off sick were excused! It was another key element to the development of the 'Police Family'.

Just before my final acceptance, I saw an advertisement in the weekly Sussex Police Routine Orders for a role based at Rye. This involved working the Camber Sands area for May to October, before moving back into Rye to cover the general sub-division during the rest of the year. This immediately appealed to me as it provided a chance to cover what was designated a rural beat and, at the same time, undertake more general policing. I discussed this with Ann as we both came from that area, as she had grown up in the village of Northiam. Indeed, we had both attended the same secondary school. It seemed an ideal opportunity for me to help my career by involving myself in a different form of policing and, at the same time, for us to return to our roots, so to speak. I applied, not really believing I had much of a chance as I was still officially within my first two years of service. I was also aware that quite a few more experienced officers were applying for the position as well. However, I was short-listed for interview and, if I am being honest, I believe that the presence of Chief Inspector Len Peters, as he was then, who had been my father's boss, undoubtedly assisted me greatly! I was offered the position and accepted it without hesitation.

Therefore, in May 1980 and still a few weeks short of the official completion of my probation, Ann and I moved to a nearly new police house next door to the main Camber Police house. My first day there was especially memorable. Whilst being shown around by PC Doug McConachie, the regular full time Camber officer, we took the police Landrover across the beach area. In the Jury's Gap area, the front wheels of the vehicle sank into a mud pool. Using shovels in the back, we attempted to dig the wheels out but the more we dug, the further in it sank! The tide was coming in quickly across the flat sands and at least we had the presence of mind to tie the tow rope from the front bumper to a breakwater structure. When the tide was fully in, the vehicle actually floated with only the police sign and blue light visible! There are many photographs held by members of the village who were very busy with their cameras that afternoon. The story was a part of local folklore for years to come. What was the follow up? The Landrover was recovered by a local company and taken to Hastings Police Station workshops where it was immediately stripped down and repaired. A local resident helpfully informed Inspector Rodney Ash, the local traffic inspector, that he had contacted Doug to say he had seen a suspicious item on the beach which required the deployment of the Landrover. Despite considerable questioning, this gentleman stuck to his guns despite the pointed questioning!

*One sinking police Land Rover!*

That first summer was a special time. I learnt so much working on my own for most of the time. Far from being an average village, the summertime population swelled to around thirty thousand, taking into account the large Pontins Holiday Village and two other holiday camps, plus day trippers visiting the famous Camber Sands. The venue has witnessed a fair number of drowning tragedies over the years and I dealt with two separate incidents involving youngsters during my time there. Whilst posted to Camber, it was also great to be given the responsibility to make my own decisions, bearing in mind that there was minimal supervision. Things were really pretty busy, and I made a number of self-generated arrests which meant I earned the respect of the local residents very quickly. I think it helped me having policed Brighton because there were not many situations I hadn't encountered there. It was also during that summer that Ann became pregnant with our first child,

Darren, who was born the following March. I also took my promotion exam to sergeant as I thought I would take advantage of the recent work I had undertaken, studying law and police procedure, as there would never be a better time to do this. However, that first winter, having moved back into Rye, I made a decision that was effectively destined to determine the direction of most of the rest of my career.

In January 1981, I started my three-month attachment to the CID, at the end of which a report was completed by the first and second line managers, determining whether or not an individual would be considered for a detective constable's role in the future. Opportunities within this period meant I was able to take on some investigations that enabled me to show that in the future I would be able to 'cut the mustard', so to speak. Again, I was lucky as I was allocated to Doug Catt, a senior DC, as a mentor. He later became my first detective sergeant when I officially started as a DC. There were also two other highly experienced DCs in the office - John Wall and Mick Poulton. I learned so much from all three guys which I never forgot. My DS was Brian Steele, a lovely man and a highly competent detective in his own right. In February, I was notified that I had passed my Sergeants exam which, whilst I was clearly not ready for promotion at this time, at least meant I had it under my belt. At the conclusion of my aide period, I was signed off as being worthy of consideration as a detective constable in the future. In my last week, I was having a drink with Brian Steele. When I arrived home, Ann was in labour and I had to rush her to the Buchanan Maternity Hospital where Darren, our son, was born a short while later. It was a very close call and Brian, bless him, was mortified that he had kept me out, having a drink that evening, and insisted on delivering a bunch of flowers to Ann the following day! Dare I say that she got used to such disruptions over the years to come!

# MY WAY

The summer of 1981 saw several events that were to change the face of policing for ever. The Brixton riots, along with similar events in Moss Side, Manchester, and Toxteth in Liverpool, ultimately led to the Scarman Report. Community leaders, politicians, academics and elements of the media all linked the riots to policing style. There was also reference to sociological issues but most saw these events as resulting from the breakdown in police and community relationships. This view had its roots in the use of police Stop and Search tactics in Brixton, as well as elsewhere. In the case of its use by the Metropolitan Police in London, the legislation used to justify this activity was known as the 'Sus Laws'. This had its origins within the Metropolitan Police Act under which officers could stop and search individuals 'on suspicion', however limited that suspicion may be. The Met were using these tactics to combat a massive increase in street robberies in Brixton, where large numbers of offenders were black African Caribbean youths. Many believed the Met Police operation, known as Operation Swamp, was responsible for alienating the police from the local black community, leading to the riots. In fairness, it was acknowledged that the black community was also suffering from sociological disadvantage, but it was felt that the two elements combined were responsible for triggering the actions of the disaffected black youth. The impact on policing of these events cannot be underestimated. As well as leading to the immediate removal of the relevant legislation from the statute books, the Scarman Report led to the creation of the most significant piece of legislation for policing, known as the Police and Criminal Evidence Act 1984. This brought into effect law and procedure which the police would need to comply with, because a failure to do so could well mean cases were discontinued at court, and action taken against officers. Its recommendations also meant the police needed to put in place forums whereby they were required to meet regularly with members of the local community and to demonstrate greater accountability for their actions. This was followed just a few years afterwards by the Broadwater Farm riots of 1985 which took place on a council-owned housing estate in Tottenham in north London. This event is mainly remembered for the murder of PC Keith Blakelock, a crime which remains unsolved to this day. The outcome was that the issues around police accountability to the local communities was reinforced once again. There have been other events since but, without wishing to diminish their importance, the ones quoted here are generally recognised as having the most significant impact on the police and are therefore responsible for much of what we see in policing today.

In terms of my own career, this carried on pretty much as it had been doing. I continued to operate at Camber in the summer months and Rye Sub Division in the winter. Kelly, our daughter, was born in March 1982 and I was about to embark on my third summer of duty at Camber. What I didn't appreciate at that time was that this would be my last as things were about to change direction for me.

# CHAPTER 3 – THE CID

❖ The Specialists.
❖ Status of the detective.
❖ The role.
❖ The detective sergeant and detective inspector years – finding my way.
❖ What it meant to me/others – a good thing or a necessary evil?
❖ The changing face/end of the generic detective – specialists within a specialism? The *we have a problem, let's create a squad* mentality.
❖ Why do people no longer want to join the CID? The death of the detective?
❖ Esprit de Corps.

In the autumn of 1982, I began my CID career at Rye. When a vacancy arose and I was offered the position, I took it without hesitation, as I had been starting to get itchy feet. I was now a little over four years into my police career, I was qualified for promotion to Sergeant and I had a young family to support and had begun to feel that, if I were to develop my career, then I needed a change of direction, and a posting to the CID presented exactly what I needed. The CID, or Criminal Investigation Department, was a step up as a police officer, although it was not formally recognised as such. Detectives were expected to operate on their own initiative for much of the time, and being given ownership of investigations meant I was able to decide for myself how best to progress these. This was exactly the challenge I needed. At this time, generally the public had the utmost respect for CID officers, and victims and witnesses had higher expectations of what a detective could achieve on their behalf. In a place such as Rye, this expectation seemed to increase, and a certain level of responsibility appeared to accompany this. CID officers in Rye were well known and addressed by their name in the street, often as not.

Whilst I had a degree of ambition, at no time did I have aspirations to hold high rank. My aims were quite modest, to be honest. My father had been a sergeant, a good one, and I felt that if I could achieve this or perhaps one more level at inspector, then that would be fantastic. If anybody had told me I would end up as Head of the CID in Sussex and that, in achieving this, I would serve in every detective rank up to and including detective chief superintendent, I would have thought they were dreaming! The man at the top when I entered the Department was Jack Reece. He was the epitome of the archetypal senior detective. He had a presence and charisma that was recognised immediately by all who came into contact with him. He was also a character and known as a straight talker and woe betide anyone who made the mistake of crossing him! I personally found him to be inspirational. He was also remembered for the manner of his driving which, to say the least, was hair-raising on occasions!

These were good days and the work was challenging and interesting. I found myself dealing with some pretty complex investigations. Of course, there was considerable experience within my office to draw on, but for much of the time, it was down to me. I have to say I relished this. Indeed, even as a junior detective, an individual was on call out of hours and, either when called out or at any other time, I, like my colleagues, was expected to advise senior uniformed officers on crime-related matters. Therefore, the extra responsibility was considerable with very little, if hardly any, additional financial rewards! However, the status gained from being seen as a specialist/expert was always enough for most of us.

Within my first few weeks, I was called out to a very unusual crime where an elderly reclusive gentleman, sitting

*A murder scene*

by his front window, was shot in the head at his home in Iden, close to the Kent border, with what transpired to be a four ten shotgun. Amazingly, he survived. It was my first involvement with a major crime investigation, with officers from other stations called in to assist. It was also my first experience of working with an incident room, albeit that we used a card index system. This method was the opposite of a computerised HOLMES (Home Office Large Major Enquiry System) set up as used today. This has been the case since the mid-1980s, following the learning that came out of the Yorkshire Ripper inquiry. This latter investigation was notorious from a police procedural point of view because the offender, Peter Sutcliffe, had come up within the investigation on seven occasions prior to his arrest. Because of the volumes involved, the card index system used was so cumbersome and unwieldy, that no significance had been placed on this. The crime committed against the old man in Iden was very unusual in nature with no apparent motive whatsoever and remains unsolved to this day.

# Kevin Moore

A funny story accompanied this incident. When initially attending the scene with Doug Catt, the DS, we obviously needed to avoid contaminating the scene around the front window which the shot had been fired into, injuring the old man. The premises were secure, and we went to the back of the house to see if we could gain access from there. There was a sash window slightly open at the top. In order to reach this, I looked around for something to stand on. There were a couple of metal buckets which, in the dark, seemed to be filled with something which I could not identify. I picked one up to turn it over by the window. Suddenly, there was an awful smell as the contents of the bucket hit the ground and poured over my hands. The smell was immediately identifiable as human excrement! The house had no sanitation and no electricity supply, and inside there were many other buckets, all filled similarly. On the way back to the station, Doug insisted on driving with me in the front passenger seat holding my hands out of the open window!

A large amount of the crime committed within the Rye area, especially during the summer months, was down to offenders from London. Many of these individuals had their own caravans located on the various holiday camps that existed in Camber and Winchelsea Beach. Some offending also involved those who came to the area as holiday makers or day and weekend visitors. By the time that many of these matters had been investigated sufficiently to identify an offender, these individuals were back in their homes within the London region. Often therefore, this would mean liaising with the Metropolitan Police in order to have people arrested. Either they would then be brought back to Rye or, more often than not, we had to travel to London to interview them in custody there. At the time, this meant that two of us would travel by car together to carry this out. I got to know my way around London pretty well as a result. It also gave me a good insight into the size and magnitude of the

Metropolitan Police. We were always made very welcome, even if at times we were referred to as 'those carrot crunchers from Sussex!' Such activities enabled me to very quickly learn to stand on my own two feet, as I often had to make decisions without direct supervision. Doug Catt may be off on rest days or annual leave and therefore decision-making was down to ourselves. I learnt to do things the correct way during my time as a detective in Rye. This meant that, in future situations where I may have been under greater pressure, I could decide how to legitimately cut corners without compromising an investigation.

I also recall a situation when Mick Poulton and I had to recover a highly valuable tapestry which had been stolen from the church in Winchelsea and recovered by Sotheby's. I remember us going for something to eat and drink with this item stored in the boot of the CID car. The police insurers would have had a fit if they had known!

During my early days as a detective, I decided to take my inspectors promotion examination. At the time, an individual could take the exam even though not yet a sergeant. I decided to do mine because, if I were successful, it got it out of the way, whereas, if left, I may never have got around to undertaking the level of studying required. I took the examination in 1984 and passed it with flying colours. I also undertook a Certificate in Management Studies at the Hastings College of Further Education. I was enjoying studying and scored very highly in the examinations on my initial CID course, finishing a very close second overall. This all served to put my name in the frame and I received a phone call from Jack Reece, Head of the CID, telling me that I should now be considering putting myself forward for promotion. He also mentioned in the same breath that I may need to test myself through working in a larger and busier environment to get myself noticed. I put myself forward for the next sergeant's promotion board but was unsuccessful. Inevitably, as if to reinforce the words of Jack Reece, the feedback was that I needed to move to a busier working environment. I had been carrying out periods of acting detective sergeant to cover periods of Doug's leave and one extended period when he had broken his ankle. Therefore, I felt confident of my abilities in this regard. As a result of the feedback, a few months later I was off to Hastings. Whilst it was a wrench to leave Rye, I did relish the challenge. It also gave Ann and me an opportunity to buy our first house as we had still been residing in our police house at Camber. It was perceived that buying a house in the Rye area would have presented potential barriers to future progression because of the distances to travel to police stations other than the one at Rye. As a result, we subsequently bought a house in the Silverhill area of St Leonards–on–Sea, and Darren and Kelly were able to attend the local primary school just down the road. I later became a Parent Governor at the Silverdale School. The make-up of the Hastings CID office at the time was interesting as, out of around sixteen detective constables, only one was a woman. This was very clearly a sign of those particular times.

After being at Hastings for about a year, I sat and passed my sergeant's promotion board and I could therefore expect to be promoted within the next twelve months. In the interim, there was a job to do. My early days at Hastings provided some opportunities to be involved in a number of murder investigations. Although there were several of these, I particularly recall the murder of a woman called Margaret Parminter who lived in Linley Drive in Hastings. A suspect was identified fairly early on, through fingerprints at the scene, the dead woman's house. The significant thing was where they were found. They were located on the walls either side of the body indicating the offender must have placed his hands in such a position to help his balance to get past the body. The fingerprints were identified as belonging to a local man named Leonard Michael Arthur Tedham. In addition to the fingerprints, a number of local drug users indicated that Tedham had disclosed his involvement in the murder to them. However, getting them to put pen to paper in a witness statement was extremely difficult. This was not only because of the state that the majority of them were in, but also because of the perceived threat posed to them by Tedham. This case highlighted perfectly a real issue that impacted on the Hastings community in the Eighties and afterwards, involving the drug scene. This was a huge problem, with the misuse of heroin, and the impact on crime levels and the general make up and fabric of the town was a major one. From a policing perspective, it always meant that we were up against it, as indeed were our partners in the Social Services and Health Departments. Crime rates involving property crime such as burglary escalated as addicts committed criminal offences in order to finance their drug habits.

In October 1986, together with a colleague Phil Waters, I was a part of the team of detectives, brought together from across Sussex, called to Brighton to assist with the investigation into the murders of the two young schoolgirls, Nicola Fellows and Karen Haddaway. This became known as the 'Babes in the Wood' murder, as their bodies had been found in a wooded area in Wild Park, opposite their homes in Moulsecoomb. Both the young girls, aged nine and ten respectively, had been strangled. It was a massive investigation which at its outset had a couple of hundred officers deployed to it, including house to house and search teams. A few months later, Russell Bishop was charged with the murders but was acquitted at court. Unfortunately, for legal reasons, I cannot expand upon details here, as Bishop is about to be re-tried for the murders. This development follows the use of recently-created legislation whereby, if new evidence is forthcoming, an individual can be tried more than once for the same crime. This has overcome the problem previously known as 'double jeopardy'. Bishop is still serving a life sentence for the abduction and serious sexual assault of a young girl, committed at Devils Dyke in Brighton and Hove, a few years after the murder of Nicola and Karen took place.

In the early part of the summer of 1987, I was made a temporary detective sergeant and moved to Bexhill CID, following an issue there regarding the alleged manipulation of crime figures. The detective inspector was made the subject of an investigation and the existing detective sergeant was moved to another post. As regards the matter involving the crime figures, this was solely down to the detective inspector involved. Often, people envisage such matters arising when individual managers are put under pressure to demonstrate improved performance which can lead to such behaviour. However, in this particular case, the person concerned was operating in this way in order to enhance his own reputation and career prospects which arguably made the situation even more distasteful. He was medically retired whilst suspended and under investigation.

I was posted there, together with the highly experienced Detective Inspector Cliff Heard. I learned a lot from Cliff in the early days at Bexhill. He was an extremely good mentor and quite properly insisted on things being done correctly. I will always remember his words to me on my first morning. He indicated that, having been promoted now, I was not being paid to be liked but to do a job and that I should 'effing well get on with it!' Harsh words on the face of it but an accurate assessment of the no nonsense approach by the man and, it has to be said, very 'old school'. I was fortunate that several investigations that cropped up over the coming weeks and months presented me with an opportunity to demonstrate my skills as a supervisory detective.

One of these involved the false imprisonment of a young girl. The case was complicated because whilst the offender was not immediately associated with the police, the victim was the daughter of a serving officer. Additionally, there were other matters which made the case more complicated because the victim was babysitting for the former wife of a police officer who had formed a relationship with the offender. There were also some relationship issues involving serving police officers linked to the various parties.

A similar thing happened a few months later when I was transferred to Hailsham CID as a temporary detective sergeant.

However, I was now starting to worry that I had still not achieved my substantive promotion. I felt that, to some extent, I was being left dangling on the end of a piece of string. The Force was going through a period where it was almost certain that my promotion would mean a return to uniform patrol as a sergeant. However, because of the events of those past months, I retained a hope that I might bypass this necessity. I was receiving really good feedback up to and including the then Head of CID, John McConnell. Sadly, John was to die unexpectedly around this time.

Then it happened. I was informed at Christmas that I would be promoted to Crawley as a uniform patrol sergeant. Ann and I were devastated. This would mean a move of house, albeit financed by the Force. However, it felt like a kick in the teeth after the work that I had been doing over the past months. Nevertheless, I gritted my teeth, put our house on the market and started to look around the mid Sussex area for somewhere to buy. Of course, the cost of housing in that area was far higher than East Sussex and this was therefore proving to be a problem. In the interim, as is often the case in such matters, the chain broke above us, thus delaying my move. Unknown to me, this was all good news as those above me were using the opportunity of the delay to make a case for me to return to Hastings as a detective sergeant, as a vacancy had just arisen there. Fortunately for me, and despite it not being within the current way of thinking, this was agreed, and I returned to Hastings CID on substantive promotion.

I was absolutely elated. To be a detective sergeant at Hastings was, in my view, a prestigious position. It was one of the busiest postings for someone at that level and it would hopefully give me a chance to shine. I still believe that the rank of sergeant is possibly the most important of all those within the chain of command structure. There is a saying which best describes the role of the sergeant. This is that there is a need for an individual holding such a position to be able to,'run with the hares and also to be able to hunt with the hounds'. This highlights the need to be able to achieve the right balance between being one of the team and at the same time appreciate the need to show appropriate leadership upwards. This can be very tricky to achieve and is a real test of the ability of the post holder to get this right. The police service relies heavily on the sergeant rank to support, mentor and drive their teams onwards in order to get things done. Without this, the organisation would undoubtedly grind to a halt.

I threw myself into my new role and was fortunate to be heavily involved in some very high-profile cases. One of these involved the murder of a member of a Hells Angel group outside the Carlisle public house by what turned out to be a rival from another group. This occurred during a late May Bank Holiday weekend in 1989. By pure coincidence, both factions arrived at the Carlisle pub late on the Saturday afternoon. A disagreement occurred and the offender, John Joseph Patrick Boyle, produced a handgun and shot the leader of the rival group from the Forest of Dean, Bruno Tessaro, through the back of his head, killing him instantly.

Following some good police work, a van containing some of the group, including the offender himself, was stopped by traffic officers at Five Ashes in East Sussex and all were arrested. I was subsequently appointed as the case officer which meant I had the responsibility for preparing the case for court. The investigation itself was highly complicated, as Hells Angel gangs do not ordinarily co-operate with the police. However, I take my hat off to the SIO who was Detective Superintendent Chris Page, who was later to become the Head of the CID himself. He made what can only be described as an inspired and yet unusual decision to bring all of the victim group back to the police station at Hastings. He ordered the restaurant to be opened, even though it was the weekend, and even allowed drinks to be purchased for them from the bar. Not too many though! He also had the foresight to appoint a dedicated liaison officer to the group long before the days of family liaison officers. PC Roy Millar was the individual chosen and what an inspired appointment it proved to be. Roy was a local beat officer, covering the somewhat notorious Hollington estate in St Leonards. He was a tough Scotsman, brought up in a challenging environment in his homeland. He was able to gain the confidence of the group to the extent where ultimately, Boyle, the offender, was picked out as the shooter by several of the victim group. This evidence was to be the bedrock of the prosecution case.

The other critical decision made by Chris Page was to liaise with the Metropolitan Police in order to ensure that the whole of the offending group, known as the London Road Rats, present in Hastings at the time of the killing, were arrested. This could happen because they had been identified through items found at the scene and in the van recovered at the time of Boyle's and his friends' arrests. Arrangements were made to have them all arrested and then interviewed by us, in order to prevent them being able to provide erroneous evidence at the future trial. During the trial held some months later, Roy Millar continued to work his magic by keeping the victim group onside in order to ensure that they gave their evidence. The likes of what was laid on from a policing perspective had never been seen before or indeed since. There was an armed police presence throughout the trial, and the traffic department provided an escort for the Forest of Dean group. It was a very impressive sight, I have to say. The ultimately guilty verdict was a testimony to those who pulled together as a team and undertook the 'hard yards' in order to gain a positive outcome and achieve justice for the victim's family and friends.

Another case that occurred around this time also springs to mind, mainly because, at the start of the investigation, there was no body. A young woman attended Hastings Police Station to report the fact that she thought her boyfriend and his brother had been involved in the murder of their stepfather. I interviewed the woman at length, and felt very early on that what she was saying had credibility, because of the level of detail that she was able to provide. Some initial enquiries revealed that the stepfather had not been seen for six months or more, although his wife, the mother of the two brothers, believed he had re-joined the French Foreign Legion with whom he had served previously. We were also able to identify a hire car which was believed to have been used in the commission of the murder and the subsequent disposal of the body, thought to be buried in as yet unidentified woodland. Having recovered the car and arranged for some initial Scenes of Crime Officer assessment by DS John (Chunky) Taylor, a test revealed the presence of blood in the boot of the vehicle. We were therefore starting to make some progress in terms of corroborating the young woman's story. I involved some more senior managers and a decision was rightly made to start a full-scale murder investigation. A team was put together, supported with full incident room capability and a decision taken to arrest both brothers in order to interview them. Early one morning, together with other officers, I attended the addresses of Ian and Vincent Skinner who lived in Hastings and Battle respectively. They were taken to Hastings Police Station and interviewed over three days, with the help of a period of further detention granted by the local Magistrates Court. Eventually, Ian Skinner broke down and confessed, whilst Vincent remained impassive. Ian eventually took us around the area before identifying woods on the Battle to Heathfield road where subsequently a grave was located and the body of the step father recovered. Ian Skinner was ultimately convicted both of murder and, along with Vincent Skinner, of preventing the proper burial of a body, an offence under the Coroners Courts Act.

There was for me a little side story to this which I never forgot and recalled it as an excellent example of man management. Detective Chief Superintendent Roger Hills, then Head of CID, had looked in on the investigation in its latter stages, just before the body was found. He asked me the identity of the young PC, tasked with looking after the offender, Ian Skinner. This had meant he was handcuffed to him for long periods, whilst the search was being conducted, including travelling around the countryside to identify the site. Roger wished to thank him personally as the situation was traumatic for the officer, as Skinner had been totally distraught, constantly crying and emotional. Chris Harrison had maintained his professionalism throughout all of this. I located Chris, and Roger Hills spoke to him. Chris left feeling ten feet tall. A lesson for us all!

Whilst a detective sergeant at Hastings, as well as supervising a team of detectives, I also had responsibility for managing what was in those days known as the newly created Special Enquiry Unit (SEU). More recently, these teams have been known as Child Protection Teams (CPT). Sussex, along with all other police forces, were required to put in place a suitable specialist response to investigate offences committed against children ie child neglect and cruelty as well as cases involving offences of physical and sexual assault. This was the outcome of what was known as the Butler-Sloss report, named after its author, Dame Elizabeth Butler–Sloss. She had been commissioned by the government in the mid-1980s, to look into the response to such matters by the Health Authorities, Police and Social Services. The decision that came out of the inquiry determined that, in future, agencies should work together to identify and investigate offences committed against children. This was to ensure that the right outcomes were achieved, with the protection of the child being at the centre of this. This work was considered ground-breaking at the time. The complexity of such matters continued to be emphasised and reinforced over the ensuing years as despite this, mistakes are still being made, as highlighted in many subsequent cases. There have still been occasions where children have been the victims of such offences and even some cases involving their death. Whilst this is abhorrent, especially in those cases where protocols have not been followed or mistakes have been made, this merely proves just how difficult a job the various agencies have in achieving a balance. Having been involved in this type of work over many years, I can state that it is often much like walking a tightrope. Wrongly taking a child away from their family is criticised nearly as much as if the child is a victim of crime and this has not been correctly identified or dealt with appropriately. The immediate response from observers is, 'How was this allowed to happen?', and similarly, 'Who is to blame?' No wonder then that professionals involved in this kind of work often feel they are damned if they do and similarly damned if they don't. I feel privileged in those early years to have worked with some excellent staff, both within my own police team as well as those working within partner agencies. I remain convinced to this day that, most of the time and working together, we did get things right on practically all occasions. As a result, I believe that a vast number of individuals committing offences against children were brought to justice, and a similarly large number of children were protected and some may even have had their lives saved.

One particular case springs to my mind, all these years later. The police and Social Services undertook the first investigation of its type involving offences committed against young boys in a boarding school in Hastings. The unique element, on this occasion compared to others, was that for the first time, certainly within Sussex, we ran a joint police and Social Services incident room. Whilst the HOLMES process was not utilised, the concepts were the same, albeit that we operated a paper-based system. The outcome of the investigation led to the headmaster, and separately a housemaster, being successfully prosecuted and sentenced to lengthy terms of imprisonment.

In 1989/1990, I had embarked on an Open University degree course. The police service was just beginning to recognise the advantages of having officers who already held a degree or were prepared to study for one. I commenced this, knowing full well I would need to fit this in with my more than full time job, as in CID we have always worked extremely long hours. Additionally, of course, there was my family to consider. I had also taken up football refereeing, having had my playing career finished early due to injury, and I was still playing cricket in the summer. Together with my great friend Robin Davies, a DC at Hastings, I had started to run a junior football team, in which Darren, my son, played. Therefore, I was going to be very busy! After two years with the OU, I found remote study difficult and opted to transfer my credits to the University of Portsmouth where, in 1990, I began a BA (Hons) Degree in Public Sector and Police Studies. I thoroughly enjoyed the course and the inputs by Doctor, now Professor, Steve Savage. I passed with a 2:1 BA Honours degree of which I was very proud. Did obtaining the degree make me a better person or in later years a better senior police officer? I personally don't think so. All it proved to me was that anybody of reasonable intelligence with the ability and self-discipline to follow a course of study can obtain a decent degree. Later on, in 2001/2002, I undertook and obtained a Post Graduate Diploma in Police Studies at the University of Sussex.

In 1990, I was made acting detective inspector at Hastings for an extended period, having successfully passed my inspector's promotion board. I still recall a couple of the questions asked, for different reasons. Firstly, my board was the day following the release of Nelson Mandela. I was asked what I thought the implications were for the Western World as a result of this action. You may ask yourself, 'What the hell has that got to do with policing?!' I found myself thinking similarly at the time but obviously must have given a sufficiently good, waffling answer to impress those board members present sufficiently to pass. The second, however, was far more relevant. I was asked by the then Deputy Chief Constable Tony Leonard what I thought about consultation. This was at a time when, probably for the first time ever, the police had started to think more about consultation and discussion and its place in decision-making. This was as opposed to the rather more directive style of management and leadership that had existed until then. I answered that I felt that consultation had its place but should never be used as an excuse by a manager for not making his or her own decision. He told me he liked my answer and I immediately grew in confidence and felt that this was indeed going to be my day! I have always tried to operate in this way over the years. Sometimes, there is time to be consultative and consider a wide range of views and options before drawing a conclusion and reaching a decision. However, policing is an operational business, and a senior leader must be able to take charge in situations where decisions need to be made and action taken, leaving no room whatsoever for doubt. Indecision leads to confusion and mistakes being made, in my opinion.

Following my period of 'acting up' at Hastings, I was posted to the then-Lewes Division as Acting Detective Inspector and whilst there in December 1990, I was given substantive promotion to Detective Inspector. I was overjoyed, of course. At what was considered to be a relatively young age, I had made DI! I went to see the Chief Constable Sir Roger Birch for the formal 'laying on of hands'. Following this, Roger Hills, Head of CID, asked to see me. He told me he felt I had the ability to sit in his chair one day. I had never considered this a possibility. I had tried to pick up the very best of the traits of senior detectives in the force, such as Roger Hills, Jack Reece, Mike Bennison, Graham Hill, Brian Foster and Chris Page, to name a few. I was confident in my own ability, but this was a real shot in the arm for me and if I needed any extra incentive to maintain my high levels of performance, then this was it. However, unbeknown to me, there was a lot of water to pass under the bridge and a lot of personal pain and suffering to take place before I was ultimately to succeed in getting there!

During my time as the Detective Inspector for the Lewes Division, I was appointed as the Incident Room Manager and based at Hastings for the investigation into the murder of Terry Daddow, who was killed in November 1991. He was shot dead with a shotgun on the doorstep of his home in Northiam, East Sussex, which he shared with his wife, Jean. This murder investigation was quite unusual and had its own elements of intrigue and complexity. Terry and Jean Daddow had both been previously married, and Jean had a son named Roger Blackman from her first marriage. Blackman was part of a group of young people who led a somewhat 'Walter Mitty' type lifestyle, centred on the Headcorn Airfield and parachuting. He had a friend named Robert Adam Bell and we were subsequently able to prove a conspiracy between Jean Daddow, Blackman and Bell which led to Bell killing Terry Daddow. Not unusually at the time and in such cases, Blackman was also a small-time drug dealer. Terry was a financial advisor and had many clients, a number of whom were elderly women. He used his undoubted charm to gain their confidence which led to large sums of commission as his reward. He also formed several quite bizarre sexual relationships with some of these women, who were clearly lonely and flattered by his attentions. Some of them made provision for Terry to benefit from their wills. This angle was a main line of enquiry in the early stages of the investigation as there was the potential for a relative of one of the elderly women to legitimately hold a grudge against Daddow as a result of what he had been doing. Terry also had a number of life insurances which, if he died, would benefit Jean to a significant extent. Local enquiries turned up a set of somewhat unusual circumstances. These involved a man who had been seen by residents hanging about in the area leading up to Terry's death. Northiam is a small village and the home of the Daddows was located in a quiet lane. Therefore, anything, such as a stranger appearing about the place, would immediately cast doubt on the legitimacy of that person's presence there. This was especially the case if it occurred during dark evenings which is what had happened in this particular case.

The man in question, when spoken to, attempted to pass himself off as somebody involved in the relocation of badger setts. He called himself Adam, and it was not long before he was identified as an associate of Roger Blackman, the son of Jean Daddow. The relationship between Terry and Roger was described by several people as being a fairly difficult one. At the same time, enquiries revealed that the relationship between Terry and Jean had been starting to break down. Terry, it would appear, had what some may describe as unusual and somewhat deviant sexual tendencies, and Jean appeared to be growing tired of these and Terry himself more generally. This provided a perfect recipe for murder. Roger Blackman involved Bell in the conspiracy and the plan was hatched which ultimately led to Terry's killing. Bell was a complex and quite plausible character to many. He had a history of fraud offences recorded against him and had secured some high-level job positions by deceiving potential employers into recruiting him. This included one large motoring company who paid him a handsome salary and accompanying benefits package, before discovering the fraud that he had committed in order to obtain the position.

At the point of arrest of the three suspects, Bell had, without appreciating how close we were to making an arrest, left the country and gone to the USA. There followed a protracted effort to secure his return. This did not include the seeking of his extradition as such a move would legally preclude his being interviewed, a key element in building a conspiracy case. Eventually, after a seemingly endless period of time and with the help of his solicitor and Bell's own co-operation, he returned to the UK. Blackman and Jean Daddow had already been arrested and bailed pending Bell's arrest. With him now safely under lock and key, the case was able to proceed and proceed it did, with all three subsequently being convicted of conspiracy to murder, and Bell of the murder itself.

As an aside to the investigation, I developed a highly professional relationship with a daily newspaper reporter which transpired to be one of the most positive experiences I had with the media during my long policing career. I shall expand on this at a later stage.

Sometime after the convictions, I was asked to attend the ITV studios in London. There was a short programme looking at the case, which included a film with actors playing key roles, including my own in providing some of the detail regarding the investigation. I was required to conduct a live interview leading up to the film itself. Live interviews are always fairly nerve-racking as there is no room for mistakes or to have another opportunity. However, it all went well, and I still have copies of the film, together with the script, as souvenirs! I also received a fee which, as usual on such occasions, was paid into the Sussex Police Welfare fund.

During my spell at Lewes Division, which incorporated the seaside towns of Seaford, Newhaven and Peacehaven, I dealt with a particularly tragic case. This involved the murder of two young boys by their mother, who was suffering from a previously-undiagnosed mental illness. She lived with her husband and their two boys in Peacehaven. Her husband was a serving soldier in the Army. He had been on a period of leave and was scheduled to return to his unit. Whilst his wife was upset at him leaving, under no circumstances could he have anticipated what was about to happen. Whilst suffering what transpired to be a severe mental health-related episode, she drowned both the boys in the bath and then put their bodies together in one of the boys' beds. She subsequently went to her father's home in Brighton and confessed what she had done and then he notified the local police. I subsequently attended the address with others to discover the distressing sight of the two dead boys. As I said previously, a particularly tragic case. The mother was ultimately rightly convicted of manslaughter as opposed to murder and was detained in a secure mental health facility.

In January 1993, I moved to Eastbourne as the detective inspector in charge of the CID team there. This was a prestigious posting and was to be the start of almost five years of the happiest and most productive years of my service. I had a great team of detectives working for me who possessed a real energy and focus on wanting to catch criminals. The division was highly successful in reducing the commission of crime generally and household burglary in particular. During a period when we were really having our greatest impact, I publicly challenged the local magistrates. In my view, far too many criminals, and in particular those involved in burglary, were far too easily securing bail after charge. This invariably meant they would use the opportunity to reoffend as they had nothing to lose as, in all probability, they would receive lengthy custodial sentences. I went to the media over this issue and there was a take up in terms of interest, both locally and nationally. Once my views were published, inevitably I incurred the wrath of the Chair of the local magistrates bench as well as the Clerk to the Justices. This led to complaints being made to the Chief Constable. My punishment was determined to be that I should attend the local magistrates' meetings in order to 'gain a greater understanding of the role and purpose of the magistrates'. I was determined, however, to stick to my guns. Most magistrates are locally appointed 'lay magistrates', as opposed to the legally qualified 'stipendiary' magistrates. The key element for the appointment of the former is for them to be able, as a locally-based individual, to take into account local problems and issues when undertaking their responsibilities. I felt that they were failing to do this and were not considering the impact of certain crime types on the local community when granting burglary offenders bail. It was a situation where ultimately the two sides were going to have to agree to differ. However, interestingly there was a significant change for the better in terms of the number of occasions where bail was granted. Additionally, I received considerable local public support. Therefore, I felt that I had successfully made my point! However, it was certainly nowhere near the last time I would voice my views publicly and face criticism from some quarters.

Whilst at Eastbourne, one of the major successes we achieved was securing the convictions of two notorious Liverpudlian brothers involved in organising much of the serious crime committed within the area. There was a considerable history of criminality involving the running of protection rackets, mainly through pubs and clubs in the town through 'the doors'. This is similar to what has been referred to in the past as operating a 'protection racket'. In these particular cases this was done through taking responsibility for the 'security' arrangements for the premises. There was also clear evidence of intimidation of potential witnesses, should they come forward. This criminal enterprise also inevitably included illegal drug supply, as well as involvement in concerted acts of violence. For many years, both prior to and following my arrival at Eastbourne, Operation Standard had been run as an approach designed to tackle this Liverpudlian-based criminality. The influx of Liverpool-born criminals had originated some years previously when benefits could be transferred from one area to another, and coincided with many individuals of dubious character deciding to set up home within the town. Of course, this does not apply to all those who may have decided to move to the area, but it was manna from heaven for those who had a criminal intent. They perceived that there was less 'heat' from the police and opposing criminal factions in Eastbourne than there was in Liverpool. It was a little like the 'big fish in a small pond' analogy for them in Eastbourne, or at least, that is probably how they perceived it. However, Op Standard was a considerable success during the time it was in place, over a period of a few years.

This intense activity to deal with the issue culminated in us securing the conviction of Peter Wynn for the murder of a doorman at the pub then known as the Sherlock Holmes. He was sentenced to life imprisonment. In this particular case, he stabbed to death a doorman working at the pub as well as stabbing another member of the public. Fortunately, the latter victim survived his ordeal. The case did have its own pressures due to the fact that I had to put in place a system in order to prevent the intimidation of the key eye witnesses. At this time, there was no recognised witness protection scheme as exists nowadays. Whilst this proved to be very onerous over the coming months, it proved to be highly successful in the end as it helped to secure the guilty verdicts.

His brother, Thomas or Tommy, was dealt with for a totally separate matter involving hate crimes committed against the family of his former common-law wife who lived in Eastbourne. He received a total of thirty months' imprisonment. The impact of these outcomes was considerable as both were in custody at the same time, and never again was their influence felt to the same extent. These convictions were secured after considerable effort to ensure that witnesses for the prosecution were not the subject of intimidation. Local measures were put in place, as a formal witness protection scheme was still in development at this time.

During my final year at Eastbourne, as the senior detective on weekend cover, I was called to what was deemed to be a 'suspicious death' at a house in Lower Park Road in Hastings. There I attended what was identified as the scene of the murder of Billie Jo Jenkins. I was to take the role of the deputy SIO or Senior Investigating Officer in the case, to Jeremy Paine, my long-time friend and colleague who was the SIO. This case has attracted considerable national media publicity over the years and has been the subject of a number of trials, re-trials and appeals. I do not intend here to give opinions and views as to the eventual outcome of proceedings against Sion Jenkins, the foster father of Billie Jo, who was ultimately acquitted of the crime. For sound legal reasons, it would be inappropriate to do so. Suffice it to say, it was a crime that formed the basis of a massively high-profile and emotive investigation. Any of my colleagues across the country who have been involved in similar types of investigation at a senior level, will understand the huge responsibility placed upon the senior investigators involved. I learned a lot about myself as a leader and as a senior detective whilst involved in this particular case. The pressures were considerable, more so inevitably on Jeremy than me. The team did an amazingly good job and undertook their responsibilities with the utmost integrity and professionalism. I had come to expect this throughout my service but none more so than at this particular time. The job of any investigation, and those involved in it, is to, as dispassionately as possible, gather the evidence and present this to the Crown Prosecution Service. It is for them to determine whether or not there is a case to answer and advise accordingly. It would be foolish of me to suggest, as an individual involved in a case, that the investigation does not impact on you and that you do not have your own views. This is only natural. However, in this country we properly pride ourselves on our administration and dispensing of justice, and many countries are envious of us in this regard. Of course, inevitably mistakes are made and sometimes the innocent may be wrongly convicted and on other occasions the guilty go free. That is just the way of things and individuals will always have their own views.

As policing has developed over the years, arguably the levels of specialism now involved has exceeded what is reasonable or viable, taking into account the need to be financially accountable. In the past, the answer with policing generally, as well as other public-sector organisations, has been to attempt to secure an increase in funding to solve a problem. Within the police, we have often been seen to respond with the creation of another specialist unit or 'squad'. If I think back to my early days in the CID, the average detective dealt with anything and everything. There was no requirement for detective units to be developed as a part of the wider CID. I suppose that the first real change came with the creation of specialist Child Protection Teams, formerly known at their inception as Special Enquiry Units, already referred to. When they started up, these were unfairly seen by some as a throwback to the days of the former Police Women's Departments. The main function of those units was to deal with all matters involving women and children. At the time of its commencement, the Special Enquiry Units were not even made up of detectives but of uniform section officers. It was only some years later that such units had their status and professionalism improved. This was achieved by ensuring that either detectives were recruited to them or that existing officers within the teams secured their detective status through training and accreditation.

My own belief is that the current plethora of distinctly separate detective units is no longer sustainable as recruitment to these will necessarily come from other areas of front line policing. I also believe that the development of this 'specialism within a specialism' has been responsible for the seeming reluctance of officers to join the CID. This is arguably because whereas, in the past, all CID officers could expect to be involved in everything crime-related, this is no longer the case. This means that often CID generalist officers have become by default not much more than processing units for individuals arrested for criminal offences by uniformed officers. As a result, there has been a decreasing ability for such officers to demonstrate their abilities as a true 'detective,' conducting their own investigations leading to positive outcomes in the form of arrests, prosecutions and convictions.

As I was approaching my retirement as a police officer and as Head of the CID in Sussex, I was contacted by the local *Argus* newspaper regarding the issue of recruitment to CID. They had picked up on the problem, highlighted nationally through the Police Federation. I was interviewed which led to a double page spread of which I still have a copy. This, amongst other things, depicts on one side a picture of myself, and on the other, an image of DCI Gene Hunt, the mythical character portrayed in the two TV series of *Life on Mars* and *Ashes to Ashes*. Many of my colleagues and staff saw this as a good opportunity to pin copies to various notice boards. I was told, tongue in cheek, that I should see this as a positive thing as they perceived me to be similar in nature to the no-nonsense detective played by the actor Philip Glenister!

Suffice it to say, I believe that policing needs to urgently review the way in which it operates in terms of crime investigation and the nature of specialist responses required. I firmly believe that we should aim to return to some extent to what existed previously for many years and arguably held its own and served its purpose. This would hopefully serve to reduce the impact on other forms of front line policing.

# MY WAY

I would summarise at this point by stating categorically that I believe I was privileged to spend so much of my police service within a detective role. Over the years, I worked with some of the very best and most highly motivated detectives operating at all levels within CID, from detective constable right up to and including detective chief superintendent, the Head of the CID. There has always existed a certain 'Esprit de Corps' within CID that is rarely apparent in other elements of policing. One could, as a detective, be seconded to an investigation in another part of the county or even the country, and quickly bond with colleagues from those different areas to the benefit of all. I guess, to some extent, historically at least, it was a little like being a member of an exclusive club and the members were proud to be a part of it.

At the end of the 1990s, the then chief officers of the force attempted to tinker around with the detective branch by renaming it the 'Force Crime Management Department'. Nobody, either inside or out of Sussex Police, really had a clue what it did! The public all know what CID is. They have seen it on television and in the newspapers. I was delighted that when I was a detective superintendent and my good friend and colleague Graham Cox became the Head of CID, he changed it back to the Criminal Investigation Department. We were therefore back to what we all knew and understood!

I do not intend in this chapter to focus on my experiences at the levels of Detective Chief Inspector, Detective Superintendent and Detective Chief Superintendent as I will cover these later in Chapter Six.

# CHAPTER 4 – PROMOTION AND RANKS – WHAT DO THEY MEAN?

- ❖ Selection processes - are they useful? Do we need them? Are they too analytical? Do they guarantee selection of the best? Place of exams? What are the risks – for and against? Is fairness an issue?
- ❖ What makes a good leader and what is leadership? – 'Liked a little, feared a little, respected a lot'. Could it legitimately be said that you are being paid to do a job, not to be liked? Tackling poorly-performing staff and the need to do this and the impact of not doing so. The leadership discussion.
- ❖ Manager or leader? - the debate. Do we need to be prepared to tell people what to do as, on many occasions, there simply isn't the time to have a discussion on the finer points of the request!
- ❖ Training.
- ❖ Was it better then or is it better now? Examples – learning from others, role models. Are we afraid to draw on the experience of the best?

The police service is quite possibly unique in terms of the emphasis and focus on promotion as a means of 'getting on'. As mentioned previously, very little, if any, recognition in terms of financial remuneration is given to specialist officers. This is despite the fact that such individuals put themselves forward for positions involving greater responsibility, which require additional training as well as hard work gaining accreditation. The public, certainly in the case of detectives, have always believed that being a detective is a promotion in itself and are aghast when informed that the contrary is the case.

As a result, to many people, the most obvious evidence of status and progression is through achieving a promotion and with it a rank. This ignores the fact that not everyone can ever hope to achieve this as there are only certain numbers of each rank required at any one time. Also, the status and emphasis placed on promotion potentially undermines those officers who, for any number of reasons, can't or don't aspire to be senior officers. Proportionately speaking, these groups of individuals will still contain many who are amongst the very best police officers within the service. Having not experienced the armed services myself, it may be that it is similar in those organisations and therefore the situation that I have described may not be as unusual as I have envisaged.

In terms of ranks within the police these are detailed as follows, working upwards in terms of hierarchy: Constable, Sergeant, Inspector, Chief Inspector, Superintendent, Chief Superintendent, Assistant Chief Constable (Commander in the Metropolitan Police Service), Deputy Chief Constable (Deputy Assistant Commissioner in the MPS), Chief Constable (Assistant Commissioner in the MPS, followed by Deputy Commissioner and Commissioner). The military have many more levels/ranks than this, of course. However, to assist understanding, Army equivalents are Captain for Chief Inspector, Major for Superintendent and Colonel for Chief Superintendent.

So, what is required in order to gain promotion? This is where it all becomes a little complex on occasions. In order to achieve promotion to the ranks of Sergeant and Inspector, the first hurdle in each case involves the passing of a nationally set examination. These examinations, in terms of their content and requirements, have varied considerably over the years. In my time it was mainly a written exam with an additional element of objective-style questions. These days, it consists of an entirely objective form of examination, together with a series of practical case scenarios or workshops where the officer responds to a series of problems presented and is assessed whilst undertaking these. There are no further examinations to be taken after these first two levels.

The next stage is then based on sitting a selection process as laid down in any particular individual force and this is applicable to all ranks or levels. This is pre-empted through the requirement to submit a written application which needs to be supported by the line managers of the candidate, together with an up to date annual assessment or more recently referred to as a PDR (Personal Development Review). Over the years, the content and requirements of these selection processes have varied considerably. In my early days, at the lower levels there were two separate interview boards. Firstly, a preliminary one and then if a candidate passed that one, a second interview, the panel of which was chaired by either the Deputy or the Chief Constable, dependent on the promotion level.

In Sussex during the 1990s, we progressed, if indeed it can be called that, to what were known as assessment centres for the levels of Chief Inspector and above. Whilst these were viewed by some as progress, as there was arguably a higher degree of objectivity involved, this development was far from universally welcomed. The system involved a candidate undertaking a series of tasks, some involving group work whilst others were individually focused. These included group discussions and chairmanship exercises on various police-related topics, presentations both operationally focused as well as topic-based, interviews, preparation of written business cases involving matters often unrelated to policing, and then mathematical and verbal reasoning tests. If successful in this process, a final interview panel then took place. One is bound to ask, of course, why this final interview was required if the assessment centre achieved what it was designed to. These processes were massively bureaucratic, time-consuming and resource-intensive in terms of their administration and assessor requirements. At the same time, they were no more 'fail safe' in terms of candidate selection than any of its predecessors. Attempts were made to streamline these by taking out some of the elements but ultimately, they were removed as a measurement a few years later.

Ultimately, many chief officers did not have sufficient confidence in the system to rely on it completely, especially in relation to selection to the most senior ranks. That is presumably why there was always a final interview board, following the conclusion of the assessment centre. Arguably, Chief Constables should be able to promote those whom they feel confident in promoting to the highest levels of their force. After all, at the Chief Inspector, Superintendent and Chief Superintendent levels, there is a need to be able to rely on the individuals operating at those levels as, day to day, they are responsible for running the Force. However, in striving to achieve fairness and equity, it was deemed necessary to put in place what was felt at the time to be a more objective form of assessment for promotion. It also created a promotion industry. At that time, we in Sussex Police actually recruited, as an organisation, a whole unit of individuals whose sole role was to administer the running of promotion systems and assessment centres. One would have to argue whether this represented value for money.

The 'fairness' debate could, if I had such a desire, develop into a whole chapter on its own. Whilst hopefully anyone of sound mind and disposition would wish to see people treated equally and fairly and avoiding any form of discrimination, it is also the case that we need to ensure, as best we can, that the right people are in the right positions. Unfortunately, in setting our sights on achieving the 'perfect' selection processes, we often perversely actually discriminate against the most able and competent. There has been considerable discussion over the past few years, both inside and outside the police service, regarding efforts to ensure that any organisation is representative of the general population. Why this should be such an issue I personally fail to understand. Those in favour of such a move argue, as an example, that the police service cannot achieve legitimacy amongst the communities we serve unless we have a similar make up within the organisation to those. My own view is that a police officer's background, in terms of gender, sexuality or race, is totally irrelevant. Being a police officer is all about serving the public, whatever the make-up that body of individuals or communities. The clue is contained within the definition of a 'constable' where reference is made to an officer conducting his or her duties 'without fear or favour'. Therefore, I would consider it to be a personal affront for anyone to have suggested that I could not deal with individuals of a different background to myself. Worryingly, in the most recent times, this has started up a debate which would actually favour ratios and positive discrimination, in an effort to achieve this. Such a move would, in my opinion, work against fairness and equity and the assurance that the best person should be appointed to a given role. In organisations where such activity has prevailed, there have frequently been individuals leave the organisation as a result. Therefore, such actions have served only to reduce the effectiveness of that agency. Inevitably, this does not happen very often at all within the private sector. The private sector is prepared to take greater risks when recruiting staff in order to achieve the recruitment of those they perceive to be the best candidates to take up any position. In this, they are prepared to challenge any resistance by employing the full weight of the law to support their cause and beliefs.

Whilst it would not be terribly scientific as a selection process, I have always felt that if you pulled together a cross section of a few highly regarded staff, they could probably select very quickly the right individuals for any particular job. Of course, there is always a need to avoid the pitfall of a 'cloning' situation developing. Sadly, over the years, attempts have been made to place such decision-making on a more scientific footing and so doing has arguably made things far too complex. In return we are actually no more certain that we have recruited the right individuals.

Inevitably, good leadership is a fundamental element of policing. A fair comparison to some extent is the Army. Much of police work involves dealing with and resolving operational problems and investigations. Most individuals who have been police officers would agree, and I am no exception, that a good leader demonstrates this attribute in an operational situation. This is when the chips are down, and difficult, swift and positive decision-making is a requirement. This is why, over the past few years, it has been so disappointing to see that less and less credit is given by senior leaders to those that possess this in spade loads. Respect is earned on the front line, not in some meeting room where there is very little risk of serious mistakes being made! I recall a quote which sadly I cannot now source which is worded as follows, 'A good leader is an individual who is feared a little, liked a little and respected a lot'. Having heard this many years ago it has led me over the years to remember these words and to keep them in the forefront of my mind. I have always felt that operational credibility lies at the heart of good leadership. Failure to be able to demonstrate sound leadership in the most challenging and difficult circumstances is, in my mind, a failure to lead. Whilst it may sound to the reader somewhat conceited, I believe that, over the years, I was able to prove myself in this regard many times over. This is actually not just about me saying this, but others who have worked with and for me, and also those who have been my line managers over the years. This was regularly highlighted in annual appraisals and PDRs (Professional Development Reviews). Operational leadership is not for the faint-hearted. The very best are often there to be shot at on occasions, and at the same time are prepared to stand up and be counted, sometimes to their own detriment. I recall a former colleague once paying me a particular compliment. He said that I, as a Senior Investigating Officer, could walk into any police station in the County of Sussex in order to run a major crime investigation. Whilst a number of officers may not personally know me or indeed I them, my reputation was such that I would be able to command their respect and co-operation. This is a similar analogy to the one that I often used when describing my view of Jack Reece, my first Head of CID. I stated that I would have been prepared to run through a brick wall for the man, metaphorically speaking, as he would not be asking me to do anything that he had not done previously himself many times before. That is a true measure, I believe, of a genuinely good leader.

The essence of success for any leader, whether they be performing the role of an SIO or other operational command responsibilities, is to be able to build a team. Without a strong team working together, there is little chance of success. This is especially the case in long-running and complex investigations. I was recently reminded of the emphasis that I always placed on involving all of those employed on a homicide or other major crime investigation, regardless of their role. This reminder came from a lady who was a typist employed on a murder that I was leading, which took place in Peacehaven in March of 2001. She recalled that she was welcomed to attend a briefing led by me which, in her past experience, was unusual. I was reminded that I had sought an answer to a question posed regarding the movement of an item in the deceased's bedroom. Being the typist, she had read all of the relevant statements and was therefore able to provide me with the answer straightaway. According to her, when I received her response, I said, 'Thank fuck for the typist!' This had clearly resonated with her sufficiently for her to still remember it to this day. What it does demonstrate to me is that every individual employed on an investigation has a part to play and therefore needs to be included. Failing to do so could have significantly negative consequences.

I also believe that too often managers think that they need to set out to be liked by all. My view of this is that, in order to do their job properly, they would immediately be setting themselves up to fail if this was their aim! I have always felt that there was a need for me to place a safe distance between myself and those whom I managed. The reason for this is that on occasions I may have had to make difficult decisions and if I were too close to an individual or individuals, then that may make the task more difficult, if the decision involved personalities. The best example that I can give to demonstrate this occurred when I was the Head of the CID. I had responsibility for five Detective Superintendents as well as a police staff level equivalent who headed up the Scientific Support Branch. I also had responsibility for an HR Manager and a Finance Manager. It came to a time when applications were being sought for promotion to Chief Superintendent and four of my Detective Superintendents applied. I turned down two for reasons I explained to them and documented. Whilst they may not have agreed or liked my decision, at least they could not accuse me of having favourites. Whilst being a manager can be a lonely place at times, to quote a former colleague and friend of mine Ian Shaw, those who decide to take 'the Queens Shilling' need to earn it!

There is another very good reason why likeability is simply not possible if one is to undertake their role correctly.

Some managers think that all they have to do in order to motivate staff is to highlight instances of good work completed by individuals and to give out awards and accolades. However, this ignores the impact of poorly performing staff. In my experience, if poor performance or behaviour is not tackled and seen to be dealt with, then even the highest performers who are in receipt of the awards will quickly become demotivated. This is simply because we all reach a point when in the workplace where, if appropriate action is not taken, there is bound to be a detrimental impact, however well-motivated an individual is. This is where respect comes into the equation. This is because all those witnessing action being taken in respect of those under-performing, including those individuals themselves, as well as those who are hardworking and delivering, will appreciate strong management.

In 2005, the then Chief Constable of Sussex, Ken, now Sir Ken Jones, held a two-day event for senior leaders within the force. One of the things that formed part of the agenda involved, on the lead up to the event, the Media Resources team interviewing and filming individuals. This related to them having been asked to articulate what they believed makes a good leader. I was myself interviewed as a part of this. Unknown to me at the time, they had also interviewed a Detective Sergeant who had previously worked for me. In my interview, I had focused on the attribute of sound decision-making. The DS had also majored on this and at the same time had given me as an example of a good decision-maker. It was amusing, and at the same time complimentary to me, that in presenting this, Media Resources placed the DS's comments immediately before mine! Following this being played back at the event, the reader can imagine the levels of leg pulling that I experienced from colleagues for days afterwards!

# MY WAY

Often, academic writers focus on a debate regarding whether leadership and management are different entities or whether they are, in fact, two sides of the same coin. I tend towards the latter. I believe that the two elements complement one another and that the best leaders are also sound managers and vice-versa, or should be. In my early days as a Detective Sergeant and then Detective Inspector, I found myself having to adapt my ways of working. I found it difficult on occasions to take a more 'hands off' approach in relation to specific investigations. This was particularly the case at Detective Sergeant level. Initially, I tended to take on investigations involving particular crime types as the case officer. For example, this may involve incidents of rape or robbery. It took me a while to appreciate that a healthy balance was required and that perhaps I would be better employed allowing members of my team to case manage such instances, with me providing direction and guidance.

Much later, in the 1990s, Sussex Police developed a very simple and yet effective definition of a leadership model to follow. This was laid out as: setting the direction, enabling and then monitoring, in order to make any necessary adjustments to the direction set. Whilst this model quickly became consigned to history as newer models were adopted, I have always found it a very useful definition to follow. To me, it provides a certain clarity which is very easy for any manager to follow and understand. As touched on previously, policing often involves operational situations where the wrong decision, or no decision in a worst-case scenario, can have disastrous consequences potentially. This means that managers on the front line need to be positive and clear regarding their decision-making. There is often little time for niceties and discussion as well as consultation. Junior officers rightly expect senior leaders to make bold decisions which, if they are correct, inevitably breeds a certain confidence within a team environment.

# Kevin Moore

As a former SIO, I believe that one of the best things to emerge was the use of a policy book or file. Another term often used is that of decision log. As a Senior Investigator leading a murder or other major crime investigation, it was not only important to record decisions taken but perhaps even more important, to document one's thought processes or 'rationale' for making a decision. This then identifies what the considerations were prior to a decision being reached. Whilst the hindsight police can question retrospectively whether a decision was a good or not so good one, there will be a sound reason for it having been made which is clearly laid down. Obviously, in less stressful situations, there is a time and a place for consultation and developed decision-making, which any good leader would be extremely foolish to ignore, as nobody has an exclusive ability to developing or thinking of good ideas.

To me, policing has always been about keeping the public safe and therefore all decision-making should have this as the ultimate aim. I remember once stating in a senior officers meeting that, unless a proposal was likely to result in 'putting more bums on seats in the cell block', then we should forget it. Now whilst this may seem extreme, the principle in my view is a sound one. If the main function of the police is to keep people safe, then a fundamental part of this is surely to lock away the criminals, as this will promote safety in the short term as well as acting as a deterrent longer term. Needless to say, such simplistic views were not always welcomed. However, I still believe that the principle involved is a reasonable one.

Leadership and management training in more recent times has tended to focus on the softer skills rather than being more operationally focused. There should always be a balance achieved, of course. A good example of this involved a problem that I had to resolve within the Scientific Support Branch. There were clear examples of poor management and supervision, outlined by those working at the operational level. I myself had to intervene to address an instance involving insubordination where a manager was undermining the head of unit amongst his peers. I involved HR in order to develop a workshop to address the issues, first of all with the staff and then subsequently with the supervisors and managers. It became very clear that individuals appointed to supervisor and management positions had been selected on the basis of their technical expertise, rather than their ability to manage and lead. In my view, there needed to be a greater balance between the two, and I was horrified to discover that the incumbents had to date received little or no leadership or management training. Therefore, the exercise that I went through on this occasion was belatedly designed to plug this gap. The counter balance to this is that, when I took up my position as the Superintendent at Brighton and Hove, I was quickly to appreciate that there was a major issue with the number of public demonstrations and large-scale events involving elements of public safety. In my early days there, I had to call upon senior Public Order Commanders to undertake the lead in the policing of these. This was totally unsatisfactory from my point of view. Due to the fact that my specialist area was major and serious crime investigation, I had never been trained and accredited as a Public Order Commander. Whilst the training in leadership and management that I had received through the Police College at Bramshill in Hampshire served its purpose, I was not equipped to undertake the roles. I therefore had to quickly enrol on a specialist training course. I was then able to take up the operational roles aligned to the matters detailed above. I will refer specifically to some of my experiences later.

Generally speaking, police training has always been of the highest quality, especially those courses involving the teaching of operational and investigative skills. I have to say that my training as an SIO was excellent and was a quantum leap forward from the past, where scant attention was paid to such matters. Learning was pretty much through experience gained on the job, so to speak.

I touched on previously the fact that I definitely consider myself to have benefited from the focus that I have given to following a number of different role models over the years. I have tried to take the very best elements of these from different individuals and have then attempted to mould these together. This applies not only to the harder skills of Senior Investigators whom I have followed on behind, but also some of the perhaps, more subtle, people skills. I learned from some of the very best senior detectives mentioned by name previously. I feel that in recent times, the term 'experienced' has, to a large extent, been consigned to history. Therefore, the value of role models and their identification has received scant attention. Sadly, no longer do many in the senior levels of the police see experience as an attribute to aspire to but rather it is potentially seen as 'old school', being a 'dinosaur' and other less than complimentary terminology. This, I believe, has in turn been responsible for a large number of mistakes and errors taking place within police forces across the country, many of which have been highlighted within the media. Why this has been allowed to happen I am not sure. However, my personal experience is that a number of senior police managers today perceive experience as a potential threat to their own authority. Rather than see such an attribute as something to protect and nurture to the benefit of their teams, they may see it as highlighting their own weaknesses in some areas. Therefore, they may feel that this may serve to undermine them in the eyes of others. I have even heard it said that experience is 'subjective'. How on earth being able to draw on numerous previous incidents and investigations can be 'subjective' is incredible. Why they can't see it for the positive aspects that most would see it as is beyond me. However, since I retired as a senior officer and took up my regional role, I can certainly say with some authority that I have indeed suffered from such views. I will refer to elements of this at a later stage. The arrogance of some who feel that they have all of the answers and are always right defies belief.

# CHAPTER 5 – STANDING UP FOR WHAT IS RIGHT

- ❖ Federation years – doing the right thing regardless. Tackling the Chief Constable! Centralisation or localisation – the positives and negatives of each.
- ❖ Discipline and Complaints/PSD – doing what is right. Challenging the status quo. Supporting the good and dealing with the bad.
- ❖ The dark days – both personal (will I ever get on?) and organisational (Sussex Police and the specific criticisms involved in the murders of Jay Abatan Jan 1999 and Richard Watson 1996 and the shooting of James Ashley Jan 1998). How past events often influence the future. Internal politics and machinations and their influences within an organisation. The Hoddinott Report.
- ❖ What does the public expect from its police service? Do we really know?
- ❖ The politicisation of policing (it started in the early 1980s you know?!) – 'Effectiveness, Efficiency and Economy,' HO Circular 114/83. The Thatcher Years and the Miners' Strike (the Lord Edmund Davies report). The Sheehy Report and David Cameron. The role of the Police Authorities and the advent of the PCCs and the role of Crime Panels – is what we have now better than before? - my personal experiences.
- ❖ 'Smaller, better, different' – Sussex Police in the 1990s.
- ❖ Bureaucratisation – the changing structure of the police service. Do we need so many support functions? Are they necessary or merely 'bean counters'? What are the things that have influenced these increases?

# MY WAY

❖ Influences on Policing – the murder of Stephen Lawrence 1993.
❖ Promotion at last!

I have always thought, throughout my personal life as well as my police career, that it was important to do the right thing, regardless of outcome, good or bad, or whether the impact personally was either positive or negative. This to me means being able to demonstrate I had a certain level of moral courage and was prepared as a result to live with the consequences of my actions or, as a senior manager, the decisions that I made. To use a well-known phrase or saying, 'If you live by the sword, you have to be prepared to die by it also'. Now I recognise that this is metaphorically speaking, but I would have to say, from drawing on my own experiences, that displaying such attributes does have its consequences, both externally in dealing with the public and other organisations, as well as internally where there may be an impact on one's career. I can honestly say also, that anything that I did or undertook which could be considered by some to be controversial, I did because it was right in my view, rather than it being an attempt to court publicity, either good or bad. I will seek to provide a number of examples when I chose to 'stand up and be counted'.

At this point, I will refer back to a previous example involving my public criticism of decisions made by magistrates. I did not do this to gain the limelight but rather because I was seeking to apply some public pressure to achieve what I believed to be the right outcome. After all, the police can keep locking up offenders but if the courts let them out to reoffend, then this is completely and utterly counterproductive. Having exhausted all other avenues and failed to achieve the required outcome, I felt compelled to use a more forceful approach, believing in my own mind that this was a reasonable response. The consequences for me on that occasion was that the magistrates decided to complain to the Chief Constable. I recognised that there may be a punitive outcome for me prior to undertaking the action that I did but I was convinced that it needed to happen for the greater good. I felt justified in pursuing matters in the way that I did as ultimately, the courts started to remand more offenders into custody which was what we wished to happen in the first place.

I have been guilty of using a saying on a regular basis and it is simply this. I believe that, at the end of a working day, I, or anybody else for that matter, needs to be able to close the front door on arriving home, believing that they have done the very best that they could have done. That was my own personal yardstick and I believed that it served me very well over the years. I always aimed to undertake my job, and the responsibilities that went with it, without deliberately setting out to 'do somebody down', especially if that somebody was a colleague. I have seen too many senior officers over the years enhance their careers through exploiting others, through either the attribution of blame or conversely claiming the credit for what others have done. I have always believed and have attempted to operate along the lines that, as a senior police officer, I should publicise the good or outstanding work of those who worked for me, ensuring that any credit due was indeed received by them. Positive actions by others would inevitably reflect well on me as their boss, if I needed that. I often felt sufficiently proud of the achievements of my staff to be able, on many, many occasions, to be able to bask to some extent in such reflective glory. The best leaders, similarly in my view, should step forward when things go wrong and take vicarious responsibility for the actions of their staff.

I suppose that, due to my views on right and wrong and standing up for my principles, it was inevitable that I would at some stage join the Executive of the local Sussex Police Federation Joint Branch Board. I was initially approached by existing officials to consider standing for the then vacant position of the representation of Detective Inspectors and Detective Chief Inspectors. For those readers unaware, each police division or specialist department has their own representative for each of the ranks of Constable, Sergeant and Inspecting ranks (both Inspectors and Chief Inspectors). Each rank has its own rank board and then separately, the chair and secretary of each rank board join together, along with the Force Federation Chair, Secretary and Treasurer, to form the Joint Branch Board. Having been elected as the CID DI/DCI representative, it wasn't long before I was elected as the Chair of the Inspectors/Chief Inspectors rank board, thus becoming a member of the Sussex JBB. This brought me into contact with chief officers, as the JBB would meet formally with them at the JNCC (Joint Negotiating and Consultation Committee), together with the local Superintendents Association and Unison. The latter represented police staff members. This was the forum where any of those bodies could raise, with the Chief Constable and his team, any particular issues relating to the policies of the force or its direction. This was a fairly difficult time in the mid-1990s for Sussex Police for reasons which I will mention shortly. This meant that often there were matters raised particularly by us, the Police Federation, which inevitably put us at loggerheads on occasions with the chief officers. As those who know me will realise, I am often the one to raise particular issues within a forum such as this one. On occasions the Chief Constable, Paul Whitehouse, would seemingly become extremely angry with me. After one particular meeting, the Chair of the Superintendents' Association, Phil Clark, declared that he had never seen the chief become so angry. The matter discussed, involved a Federation view that the then-sixteen divisions within the

# Kevin Moore

County were being operated as separate 'fiefdoms' by their respective Superintendents and that there was very limited corporate identity any longer. The Chief seemed to disagree with this view! The point that I was attempting to make, on behalf of the local Federation, was that the leadership for the Force did not seem to be coming from the Chief but rather relied on the whim of individual Superintendents. Whilst there is always a need to allow initiative linked to local need, the general direction should be coming from the 'Centre'. I had the temerity to suggest that the Chief was guilty of not following his own leadership model ie setting a clear direction, enabling and monitoring/adjusting etc. In my naivety, I suppose that the sense of justice that I felt following the meeting, about the way in which I had presented the issue, took precedence in my own mind over any career aspirations that I may have harboured at this time. However, once again, I felt that it was absolutely the right thing to do.

I had no issue with a local focus in terms of the point of delivery of service, in this case policing. However, when there was a danger in a County Force of the public receiving a different service for a similar request, dependent upon what part of the County they were in, then this in my opinion was totally wrong and I said so! It amounted to a form of 'post code lottery' in my view. There were a number of other occasions where it could be said that I was definitely not flavour of the month, and the magistrates matter was just one of these! I was also operating fairly frequently as a 'Federation Friend'. This involved representing officers in situations involving misconduct investigations, undertaken in those days by the Discipline and Complaints Department (D&C) now PSD (Professional Standards Department). In cases where there was no threat of an officer losing their job, the friend acted similarly to a solicitor and spoke for the accused officer, including instances where the officer contested the allegation. In the most serious of cases, where a Chief Constable's hearing was the outcome, then the role became one similar to that of a solicitor's clerk, through supporting the solicitor appointed through the national Federation office to represent the accused officer. I had a number of successes in terms of what I felt to be justifiably unproven cases. Of course, this probably did nothing to enhance my career prospects at the time either.

One of these involved a Sergeant who was accused of making a racist comment to a female officer working on his section. He was also accused of failing to properly supervise and deal with a PC on his section who was subsequently dismissed for a catalogue of fairly serious disciplinary offences. The case which resulted in a Chief Constables disciplinary hearing led to the first matter being found unproven. The second matter, whilst proven, was heavily mitigated in this Sergeant's favour. This was because the PC concerned had been a major problem historically and it could therefore be shown that failures to deal with him previously meant that this Sergeant was by no means the only blameworthy supervisor. He kept his job as a result.

There was an irony to my involvement with the fighting of others' causes, because, in November of 1997, I was transferred to the Discipline and Complaints Department, now known as Professional Standards. This was not necessarily a move that I had either sought or indeed wanted. It involved a complete shift from poacher to gamekeeper, in a manner of speaking! However, as things ultimately turned out, it was a move that did me a lot of good, both personally as well as professionally. I had been involved in a number of instances involving professional differences of opinion with my then-Superintendent. I am pleased to be able to say that in more recent times, he and I have resolved any issues that we may have had with one another at this particular time. I recognise that my personality is such that, at times, I am not the easiest person to deal with. I have strong views and opinions and if an individual possessing such traits comes up against a like-minded personality, then inevitably fireworks may result! Sadly, this is what happened between that particular Superintendent and myself. It was sad really because I had always had the utmost respect and liking for him, as he indeed had for me. However, with him holding the position that he did, there was only going to be one winner! I was too blind and set in my ways to appreciate this at the time and in effect, I ended up bringing about my own downfall, arguably through my own pig-headedness. Later, I was to come to appreciate, albeit belatedly, that there are occasions where one has to be prepared to lose a battle in order to win a war. Whilst holding the rank of Inspector, I could wield a considerable influence over those for whom I had a direct responsibility, but my levels of influence would never extend beyond this. I therefore needed to adapt my style and way of doing things so that, whilst I did not necessarily change inwardly, outwardly at least I was seen in a different light. This realisation was to come a little later.

However, I had a great time at Eastbourne. The period was hugely successful for me both personally as well as for the Division and the CID office specifically. The results achieved were simply outstanding. The detection rates, especially for burglary and drug-related crime, soared and we locked up a massive number of criminally-minded individuals. One particular case stands out for me. We had experienced, over many months, a series of armed robberies/aggravated burglaries of sub post offices in the area. The offenders would break into the post offices in the early hours of the morning, tying up and pistol-whipping victims who lived on the premises. They could then gain access to the safes to steal large quantities of cash. A long and protracted investigation led to us identifying a number of suspects. Early one morning, we executed a number of search warrants leading to the arrest of the three main subjects. We recovered a number of hand guns, sawn off shotguns and even a recommissioned sub-machine gun. The offenders received a total of forty years' imprisonment between the three of them.

I was privileged, during my time at Eastbourne, to have a number of excellent detectives within my team who were highly motivated and experienced. We worked hard and enjoyed a few beers from time to time in the police social club at Eastbourne Police Station. Happy days indeed!

It was not always a story of success, however. I recall two matters which I hope demonstrates the fact that I, like any other, have my own failings! Each has its own funny side. Firstly, there was a case involving an investigation into allegations of drug dealing. With the assistance of the local divisional Drug Unit, my team had identified three addresses at which we decided we would execute search warrants early one particular morning. There was nothing unusual in that as it was something that was regularly undertaken. As I held the necessary rank, I gave my authority for officers to seek to obtain the necessary warrants from the magistrates. We held a briefing prior to the execution of the warrants and the teams went out to get on with the job. Sometime later I was contacted to be told that we had entered the wrong premises in relation to one of the addresses. Doors had been damaged in securing entry which is not unusual. However, sadly the addresses had clearly got mixed up because the premises in question belonged to one of the informants giving us the necessary information to justify the course of action taken in the first place! What made it even worse was the fact that the informant was an elderly lady who at the time was the Chair of the local Eastbourne Business Women's Group! She was an upstanding member of the community and we had forcibly and mistakenly entered her home!

I went and purchased a large bunch of flowers and visited the poor lady involved. However, she rightly made a formal complaint. When Discipline and Complaints undertook their investigation, it was pointed out to me that the most effective way of dealing with the matter was for me as the officer authorising the securing of the warrants to take full responsibility. This is exactly what I agreed to do, and I was duly admonished and an entry to that effect was recorded in the local divisional discipline book. I made sure however that those responsible for the 'cock up' bought me a few drinks up at the bar!

The second matter led to Sussex Police's Buildings and Estates Manager threatening me with prosecution for criminal damage! This was as a result of a long winded and tiresome effort I had made to make some structural changes to the CID office at Eastbourne Police Station. I wanted to develop some office space in order to create a local crime management office to house the CID clerical staff in order for them to be able to better undertake their responsibilities. Sadly, one weekend in my absence, some of my team took my frustration with the lack of progress literally. They brought in some tools and started to take down stud walls and commence the work needed. They made a right mess and there were six-inch nails hanging out of walls and the flooring thus making the whole environment dangerous and uninhabitable.

To compound the situation, I was due the following week to be interviewed by BBC television regarding the policing of Eastbourne. They got to hear about the story of the building issue and of course I delighted in giving my honest opinion regarding the levels of bureaucracy faced in order to get things done in an effort to make progress. This when broadcast inevitably upset many and resulted in a site inspection being undertaken by the Estates and Buildings Manager the following day. It was then that my Superintendent, Kit Bentham, was told that my behaviour had been irresponsible and was tantamount to me having committed criminal damage. As a result, I received another rebuke! It was worth it in some ways though because the work needed was undertaken straight away. However, I did have to eat a considerable amount of 'humble pie' and I did accept that I should not have allowed things to happen in the way that they did.

I spent two and a half years working in the Discipline and Complaints Department and it was to be a real eye opener. It also coincided with my being promoted to Detective Chief Inspector. More especially, it was also during my time there that things happened within Sussex Police that were destined to change its direction completely. As a bi-product of this, it was also to change my career significantly in a positive sense.

From a practical perspective, although I had failed to appreciate it at the time, I needed a change of direction, as I had been at Eastbourne for almost five years and had arguably become too comfortable and required a fresh challenge. Separately, the work of that department showed to me the importance and need for professionalism and integrity in any organisation and individually within its members of staff. When I started my role, I had always believed that the over-riding proportion of the Force comprised of hard-working, honest and professional individuals. Whilst I am pleased to say that this view has not changed, it does not hide the fact that there are, as in any organisation, some bad and often corrupt individuals who can quickly undermine the integrity of that agency. At the conclusion of my time there, I was grateful to move away from that type of work. It would be fair to say that I had started to develop a huge sense of cynicism regarding the motives of police officers, as well as complainants, due to the things that I came to be involved in. What I now appreciate looking back is that the ethos and reason for being of any organisation can often influence the way in which its work force operates. Lax management and leadership regimes can contribute to a more liberal approach to discipline. I believe that this was the catalyst for the wrongs that I encountered during the two and a half years that I worked within Discipline and Complaints. Going back to my earlier comments regarding my attempt to raise the issue of a lack of centralised control at the JNCC meeting, I firmly believe that this was a factor in terms of cause and effect.

I do not intend to discuss here specific investigations or individual officers involved, as I believe that such action would be both morally wrong, as well having potential legal implications. Suffice it to say that, as difficult as the work was, I was pleased to be able to play my part in removing some individuals from Sussex Police who to my mind brought the Force into disrepute through their actions. I was amazed by the behaviour of some individuals and the total arrogance that they displayed. These people appeared to operate in a manner which suggested that they felt that they should be able to operate outside of the organisation's boundaries, with absolutely no comeback on them. To me at least, they were no better than some of the criminals dealt with by the police. The service was well rid of such individuals. It is too easy in my mind to trot out the oft-used phrase that the police service is the public and therefore the public is the police. That should never be used as an excuse for the poor behaviour of some. To me, whatever the circumstances, the police service, and those within it, need to be better than anyone else in terms of their behaviour and should always be beyond reproach. Anything less has the potential to cause irreparable damage to the reputation of the organisation.

What the work also enabled me to achieve was to ensure that genuine mistakes made by officers in undertaking their duties were identified and dealt with appropriately, without a detrimental impact on the officer or officers concerned. Sometimes in trying to do the right thing, mistakes are made as regards strict adherence to policy and procedure. Also, crucially, on many occasions, I was able to show that a complaint made by a member or members of the public could be false, malicious or exaggerated. Therefore, I was able to demonstrate and prove the innocence of officers on occasions to the then-PCA (Police Complaints Authority) which was to become the IPCC (Independent Police Complaints Commission). I would have to say that this brought me as much personal satisfaction as dealing with the guilty.

Police officers sometimes believe that Professional Standards are out to get them and similarly the PCA or IPCC, and the public view Discipline and Complaints or Professional Standards as instrumental in unjustly supporting police officers. Investigating officers are therefore often damned if they do and similarly damned if they don't!

During my early days in Discipline and Complaints, in fact in January 1998, I was called out, along with another officer, to take initial action in relation to the police shooting leading to the death of James Ashley at his flat in St Leonards-on-Sea. We knew that, due to the seriousness of the incident, the PCA would ultimately take responsibility for the investigation. Also, they would subsequently instruct a force other than Sussex to undertake this, under their direction and supervision. Our job therefore was to secure any immediately-available evidence prior to Kent Police, as was subsequently to be the case, taking over. I interviewed and took an initial account from the girlfriend of the deceased. Ashley, a Liverpudlian with a criminal history, had moved to Sussex a number of years previously. He had originally been resident in Eastbourne, prior to moving to Hastings. The local police had been conducting a covert investigation into what intelligence sources suggested were Ashley's illegal drug dealing activities. Some key intelligence suggested that Ashley was in possession of an illegally-held firearm. This led to an armed police response in an effort to arrest Ashley and secure the firearm.

This required the identified police commander for the incident determining the tactics that would be employed and the methodology involved, in order to neutralise the threat posed.

The outcome of this operation is now a matter of public record. Armed officers entered the flat lived in by Ashley and his girlfriend in the early hours of the morning. The officer firing the fatal shot, and a number of others involved in both the firearms response as well as the development of the intelligence leading to this, were the subject of criminal charges and were acquitted at the subsequent trial. The officers concerned were all ultimately allowed to return to duty following the finalisation of all proceedings, including the conclusion of internal disciplinary matters overseen by the PCA. However, whilst in the short term the officers returned to work after many months away, they never recovered from their ordeal and were the subject of medical retirements.

This, however, does not by any means tell the whole story or indeed describe the fall out that ensued, in terms of the impact upon Sussex Police as an organisation. This would eventually include the medical retirement of the Deputy Chief Constable Mark Jordan, and ultimately the premature retirement of the Chief Constable Paul Whitehouse. These were to be dark days for the Force which for many years had played and would continue to play such a huge part in my life. As well as the investigation undertaken by Kent Police in relation to the shooting itself, a decision was taken by the Sussex Police Authority, following influence from the Home Office level through the Home Secretary David Blunkett, to conduct a separate and unrelated but linked investigation. This would be led by Sir John Hoddinott, the Chief Constable of Hampshire. He was a hugely charismatic man and also an individual who possessed massive gravitas and integrity. His terms of reference involved looking into the actions of the chief officer team of Sussex Police which was linked to their actions and involvement in the fatal shooting of James Ashley. The major issue leading to this had involved the Chief Constable's statement made during the morning following the shooting itself. He had publicly gone on record in the media to give his full support to the officers involved in the incident. Arguably, and indeed that was how the family of Ashley viewed it, he had, through his words in their minds, effectively exonerated the officers of any blame. Not only were the family distressed regarding his stance, clearly the PCA were also far from enamoured, as arguably he had effectively undermined their investigation in the eyes of the deceased's family as well as the wider public. Why he responded in the way that he did only he will know. Seen in its best light, it was naïve in the extreme.

The Hoddinott investigation was to have far-reaching effects indeed. I was one of a number of officers interviewed by him. He was an extremely thorough and inquisitive investigator. Not only did he wish to understand my role and involvement in the aftermath of the shooting, he sought my views and opinions, backed up with evidence, regarding the actions of others. In a wider sense, he also wanted me to give my opinion on the chief officer regime in Sussex at the time.

Again, and quite properly, he not only expected an answer, but he wanted it to be supported with sound evidence. There was a feeling of real pressure and accountability on the part of all of those interviewed. There was at the time, it is fair to say, a perceived influence exerted by a number of senior officers within the force who were viewed as being part of a privileged group. It was felt that the group could influence promotions and would regularly meet in a particular public house in mid Sussex where such discussions took place. Whatever the full truth of the matter, only those who were a part of this group will be able to say.

This issue, in its broadest sense, formed a part of the questioning that I certainly, and others obviously without my knowing, faced. As those who know me would expect, I told the truth as I saw it, supported with evidence. At the end of the interview, which lasted a number of hours, I felt as if I had been 'put through the wringer', so to speak. Having spoken to others who were interviewed, whilst not discussing the content of their interviews, I am aware that they experienced similar feelings.

At the same time, the Force was also experiencing severe criticism, arising out of reviews undertaken by Essex and the Metropolitan Police respectively. These reviews were related to the murder investigations involving Jay Abatan, outside of the Ocean Rooms night club in Brighton, and the businessman, Richard Watson, in the garden of his home in East Grinstead. The bottom line was that the Force had failed to investigate these in accordance with national policy and guidance laid down relating to practice and procedures. Whilst these matters in themselves may not have ultimately affected the outcomes of those investigations, if taken as a whole together with the shooting of James Ashley, the perception was that Sussex Police was a failing force. This was not helped by the fact that, in terms of those areas subject to performance measurement and comment at Home Office and Government level, Sussex were performing poorly when compared to similar forces.

It was against this backdrop that suddenly, senior detectives were in vogue so to speak. Ironically, I had decided that, under the regime in existence at this time, I would not submit myself to the rigours of the promotion system again. I had been a Detective Inspector for nine years and it was beginning to look as if I would end up being one of the longest serving DIs in the history of policing! I had decided that I could not sustain another attempt, only to fail once again. I equated it at the time as being similar to an analogy whereby I stood in front of a promotion assessor with my legs apart, pointing to my private parts and stating, 'Kick me here as hard as you like as it really doesn't hurt me'. The truth however was entirely different because psychologically, the annual failures were becoming more and more difficult to recover from. However, I was advised that this particular year, 1999, was to be the year of the detective. The Force appeared to be in dire straits following all of the criticism relating to the mistakes made in major investigations. This led to a view that the time had come to promote individuals with the necessary experience to take on such roles. However, I still needed some convincing but ultimately decided to 'throw my hat into the ring' once again.

During the assessment centres, from which successful applicants would progress to an interview board, I honestly did not feel that I had performed as well as on previous occasions. The 'game playing' in such environments was simply not me and I hated every minute of the falseness of it. However, I succeeded in getting through to the interview. I always knew that I would perform well in an interview as I have always believed that you see the real person in such a setting. There is no hiding place in an interview situation and you stand alone on your own merits. I skated it by all accounts and therefore I was to be promoted to Chief Inspector. Indeed, I was immediately made DCI in Discipline and Complaints, pending my release to take up the DCI position in the Investigations Branch within the Force Crime Management Department, better known and soon to be renamed as HQ CID.

In this latter role, I would be one of the Force's Senior Investigating Officers, as well as having a day job looking after force policy in relation to Child Protection and also the Force Fraud Investigation Unit. Therefore, I had at long last achieved my promotion after much pain and suffering. However, I did not lose sight of the fact that this had only happened because of the circumstances prevailing at the time. I always felt that the promotion probably caused the Chief Constable considerable personal angst as I recognised that I was certainly not one of his favourite people! I also did not harbour any realistic thought of further advancement under the existing regime as a result. Little did I know that, within a very short space of time, things were going to change radically within Sussex Police and I was to personally benefit from this.

At this juncture, as I have reached the point where I was due to leave the Discipline and Complaints Department, I believe that it is worthwhile discussing in general terms the issue of the investigation of complaints made against the police. The vast majority of complaints made by the public are investigated internally by that Force's own Professional Standards Department as they are now known. A certain number of the most serious are either supervised by the now IOPC (Independent Office for Police Conduct) or undertaken as investigations solely by them. This has not always been the case, however. During my service, there have been a total of four different iterations of organisations overseeing the investigation of complaints made against the police. Initially, at the time that I joined, there was the PCB (Police Complaints Board). This was subsequently replaced by the PCA (Police Complaints Authority). This then became the IPCC (Independent Police Complaints Commission) leading to the most recent version, the IOPC.

The differences between the various models really involves the level of resourcing and jurisdiction. In the first two versions, the bodies concerned were made up of members who oversaw all investigations completed by police officers, and signed these off in terms of decision making at the conclusion. This could involve matters which were agreed to involve complaints that were unproven or unfounded, right up to those potentially involving criminal allegations against police officers. It also involved those cases where a decision was made that an officer should face a discipline tribunal or misconduct hearing. In these cases, if proven, an officer could face sanctions escalating in severity from a reprimand right up to and including dismissal from the service without notice. However, all investigations were undertaken by force departments, either in their entirety or under the supervision of the PCB and PCA. In the most serious of instances, the PCB or PCA could appoint an independent force to undertake the investigation. The more recent versions of the IPCC and IOPC have a standing army of staff able to investigate the so called higher end matters totally independently from the police. Each force still had its own PSD to deal with lower to middle tier investigations.

The effectiveness of the various versions has always been a bone of contention for police officers on the wrong end of such matters, as well as members of the public. The latter may be involved either as a direct complainant or as family members of an individual who may have died through their contact with the police. Examples of this include individuals shot dead by armed police officers, those who had died in police custody, or deaths which occurred during the course of a police pursuit. There are other variations of these which, for my purposes here, there is little value is detailing as this may simply confuse those reading this. These in the main involve either direct or indirect contact with the police where a death has occurred. Whatever version of complaints investigation has been in existence at the time, it would be fair to say that there has been very limited satisfaction expressed by either the public or the police. Investigations are often extremely lengthy, leaving both complainants and their families, and of course police officers, in a state of limbo, often for periods of many months or in some cases, years. It does not seem to matter how many resources are thrown at the problem, the same issues appear to persist. There have been endless changes to processes and the manner in which complaints are recorded and investigated, as well as the police disciplinary code or code of conduct and the various outcome and sanctions linked to matters found to be proven. My own belief is that there is a simple problem linked to all of this. The very best investigators are those who undertake such matters as a part of their day to day work over many years and are involved in investigating the most serious crimes and the criminals involved in committing them. These investigators, by definition, are most likely to be either current or retired police officers. The authorities have tried to employ individuals from other organisations and agencies such as the Post Office, the DHSS etc. However, with no disrespect to those individuals, the simple fact is that they are not sufficiently skilled to undertake the type of work involved and have not investigated cases of the magnitude we are discussing here. In trying to demonstrate independence from the police by recruiting non-police officers, the authorities involved have almost perversely in effect set themselves up to fail.

# MY WAY

I can quote a good example involving myself to demonstrate my point. In early 2009, having made my intentions known regarding the fact that I would retire as a police officer in the September of that year, Martin Richards, my Chief Constable, had been approached by an agency involved in recruitment on behalf of organisations. In this case, the IPCC, as it then was, were looking to appoint an individual to a new position of Director of Investigations. This agency contacted me, and I had a long telephone conversation with an individual at the conclusion of which he stated that I seemed to have all of the skills and attributes required for the role. Time was short, and I had no real time to consider whether or not I really wanted the job, because the deadline for applications to be received was only days away. I therefore submitted my application and I was given an interview. During the course of the interview, the panel only seemed to want to focus on how the public might perceive the appointment of a retired senior police officer to the role, taking into account the need to demonstrate independence. The fact that I was a highly experienced and successful investigator and had been involved in many high profile and complex investigations did not seem to matter. Also, my experiences as a senior leader and manager didn't seem to register in any meaningful way either. Suffice it to say, I didn't receive a job offer. Ironically, and as I told the person who contacted me regarding the outcome of the interview, I had already decided that, even if I had been offered the position, I would have declined it. The way things have gone with the IPCC, I would have to say that I am extremely pleased that I did not end up working for them. It just seemed to me that they were completely bogged down with the whole issue of 'independence' rather than recruiting the right people into their organisation. Rightly or wrongly, I viewed their stance as casting some doubt on my personal and professional integrity. This is because I have always operated independently in whatever investigation I have undertaken. In addition, I believe that my track record whilst I served in the Discipline and Complaints Department amply demonstrates this very point.

To my mind then, even as we speak, the investigation of complaints against police officers continues to be flawed in my opinion. This will continue to be the case until such time as somebody in a position to be able to influence things wakes up to the fact that the best investigators are police officers. Additionally, I believe that the 'poacher turned gamekeeper' analogy applies here. Who knows best how police officers think and react, both in a positive or negative sense? It is not rocket science!

I always felt throughout my police service that I knew what the public expected of its Constabulary. But there have been times when I have not been as certain. I suppose inevitably, in whatever way one looks at things, the vast majority of the public are often the least vociferous. Therefore, it is often difficult to gauge whether the level of service provided is good or at least satisfactory. Unless an individual has a need to seek the assistance of the police, then I guess that it is quite difficult for them to determine whether or not the police service is doing a good job. Similarly, it is also too simplistic for an individual to decide what they require in totality from an organisation if they have only accessed one small part of it. As a result, the police service has often been accused of deciding for itself what it is that the public want.

In relation to this, I don't suppose that the police are unique. After all, we are the professionals and that is what we are paid to do. I think that there is probably a sensible balance to be achieved. I have personally always used what I refer to as the 'Mrs Moore analogy' as my yardstick, with reference to my wife. What is it that she, as an ordinary

*Mrs Moore!*

member of the public rather than being the wife of a police officer, wants from the police service? Having previously tested this on her, I think that I am pretty well able to state that she wishes to be kept safe and equally to actually feel safe. She also wants to know that she can call upon the police if she needs to and that they will respond positively. This second point is more about reassurance and this is often difficult to measure. The public, and therefore Mrs. Moore, expect us to deal professionally with incidents requiring the attention of the police. Additionally, there is a proper expectation that we will remove the really bad people from the streets and, with the support of the judicial system, lock them up. I suppose a similar saying that fits in with my personal analogy is the 'Man on the Clapham Omnibus'. In other words, what would the average man or woman justifiably expect from their police service? I believe that, using this as a measure, things do actually become much clearer. It really isn't that difficult or complicated. Therefore, the position taken by Sussex Police in the late 1990s, I believe, mitigated against those serving to be able to achieve this.

There was a slogan at that time within the Force known as, 'Smaller, Better, Different'. I recall in later years that, if you were stupid enough to mention this phrase within the presence and hearing of Sir Ken Jones when he was Chief Constable, it was probably sufficient to send him into a state of apoplexy! At this particular time, technology and computer systems were starting to come to the fore. There was a view within Sussex Police at senior level that, if we majored on technology, we could reduce the numbers of police officers and staff that we needed to have in place. To cut a long story short, the overall establishment of police officer numbers was reduced by over two hundred. In a force of under three thousand officers, the impact was considerable. More importantly, this occurred at a time when our neighbouring forces were increasing their numbers of police officers and therefore we were the ones out of step.

This 'whim' was to have considerable impact in the future because, a few years later, in times of high recruitment, Sussex failed to equalise its numbers in line with our neighbours in Kent and Hampshire in particular. These forces were responsible for policing similar-sized communities to our own in Sussex but had significantly more officers than we did. In later years, when central government cuts were made, this meant that Sussex suffered disproportionately compared to our neighbouring forces. The only way available to counter this would have been through major increases in the council tax precept for policing. Whilst in the richer areas such as Surrey this did not pose a problem for police authorities and more recently

PCCs (Police and Crime Commissioners), the same could not be said for Sussex. The impact of this has been considerable in recent years with police officer numbers being reduced considerably. The irony of the situation in Sussex in the late 1990s was that at that time, there was no pressure being applied either locally or nationally to make savings. Quite the opposite in fact. Recruitment across the country was considerable and we were the ones moving in the opposite direction. This sadly is not the case in more recent times. Most people who work in any arena involving service provision would struggle, I would think, to agree with the maxim that 'smaller' can ever be 'better'. However, most would agree that it is most definitely different!

The alleged 'politicisation of the police', has been the subject of considerable discussion and academic comment over more recent years. The police are 'servants of the Crown' and are therefore not employees in the strictest sense. To this day, police officers are not permitted to strike. As a result of being Crown servants therefore, the neutrality of the police has always been a given historically. However, is this still the case today? Academics have argued that the police have never been truly apolitical. In terms of historic accountability, the county and borough forces were answerable to bodies known as Watch Committees made up of local high-profile individuals and councillors. Subsequent to this, Police Authorities were responsible for overseeing their local forces and holding Chief Constables to account. Originally, the set-up of these was tripartite in nature with local councillors, local magistrates and independents making up the governing group. Therefore, there was a clear element of political influence potentially.

When the Conservative and Liberal Democrat coalition Government took power in 2010, they were keen to address what they perceived to be a lack of accountability of police forces to their respective police authorities. This issue had already been on the Conservative Party's agenda for quite a while. As a result, we witnessed the birth of the Police and Crime Commissioner. However, the thinking behind this was flawed, I felt, as, far from bringing about greater accountability and less political influence, the converse has been the case. In the first round of PCC elections held in November 2010, a large number of independent, non-politically affiliated individuals were elected. However, this situation was reversed in the more recent elections in the summer of 2015. The vast majority of PCCs are now members of a main political party and many of these are Conservatives. One of the more controversial outcomes of the 2012 elections involved some PCCs who appeared, quite deliberately, to set themselves up for a confrontation with their Chief Constables. This led to a number of unseemly fall outs with a number of Chief Constables leaving their posts early. Of course, and inevitably, the Government attempted to pass this off as the PCCs demonstrating they were holding Chief Constables to account, as envisaged at the outset. However, this ignored the fact that most of the resignations seemed to originate from personality clashes, rather than professional differences of opinion. It did not assist the situation that a number of the new PCCs were retired police officers who in some cases appeared to operate in a manner suggesting that they felt that they had a point to prove. The whole thing was arguably very unseemly.

The Crime Panels, employed to hold the PCCs to account, appear to be totally and utterly 'toothless'. This has been emphasised through a number of high-profile resignations by individual members of some of those panels who stated that they felt that the role of the latter was powerless to intervene in any meaningful way.

I believe it would be correct to say, drawing on my own experiences, that perhaps historically, the original police authorities to some extent paid lip service to their responsibilities. Their relationships with Chief Constables could on occasions be described as fairly cosy and therefore there was limited accountability in place. However, in the 2000s, when the make-up shifted away from magistracy membership and there were only councillors and independents, things were very different. My personal view is that those individuals took their roles very seriously indeed. In Sussex, individual members of the Authority were aligned to specific police divisions and departments. As both a divisional commander and then as the Head of the CID, I can state categorically that the individuals working with me were very intrusive. They quickly developed a thirst for knowledge in an effort to make them more effective in their roles. The Police Authorities were also considerably cheaper in terms of the public purse than the current PCC set up. Members of the Police Authorities were only entitled to receive expenses and were therefore not in receipt of any other form of remuneration. They were supported through provision of a back-office function led by a Chief Executive to the Authority, along with a number of administrative posts. However, today, PCCs are salaried and they have a whole entourage of support including a number of highly salaried executive positions.

In terms of the wider argument regarding whether or not the police have been politicised, the actions of Chief Constables in recent years have served to suggest that they are very much in the mould of being political animals, in my view. One needs to be careful not to ignore the past and to consider whether this may have always been the case. I believe that, as with many things in life, much depends on individuals. I believe that in the past there have been a number of politically motivated chief constables. However, during more recent years, I also feel that in Sussex one or two were less inclined to operate in this way and indeed wished to distance themselves from such involvement. I saw this as a positive thing and therefore I hope that I will not upset them by saying that I believed this to be the case with both Ken Jones and Joe Edwards. I always felt that they were what I would describe as 'proper police officers'. By this, I mean that they were more motivated by the operational aspects of policing, rather than the political side of things. As such, they were accorded a certain level of respect by the rank and file officers. Joe Edwards for many years held a leading position regarding the ACPO (now NPCC) port-folio for the police operational use of firearms. Ken Jones had held the port-folio for Counter Terrorism. Both of these roles have a hugely operational element to them. This is an interesting point in itself because, during their regimes, the performance of Sussex Police came to be recognised as being amongst the very best in the country. Indeed, we were held in high regard by our peers and were located in the upper quartile of forces in terms of delivery of the key performance indicators set by the Home Office at the time. However, and despite this, the local great and the good may have preferred a different profile to be adopted by their Chief Constable. I do believe that this helps to explain the different appointments made over the years of Chief Constables. If a job needs to be done in terms of there being a requirement for a force to be pulled up by its boot laces, then the likes of Sir Ken and Joe Edwards were the men for the job. If things were ticking over and there were no adverse issues surrounding the Force, then perhaps a different style is needed. This matter is a very subjective one as it is very much opinion-based as to what provides the better solution. Probably, the operational cops would prefer the former approach whilst the 'thinkers' would be more likely to favour the latter.

The real argument regarding the politicisation of the police probably has its foundations in the 1980s more than at any other time. There were a number of events and situations that were responsible for bringing this about. Firstly, as previously discussed, there were the riots in Brixton, Manchester and Liverpool, leading to the report prepared by Lord Scarman in 1981. This was probably the first occasion whereby politicians sought to influence the behaviour of the police as an organisation through the questioning of tactics used by the latter. This, unlike today, was exceedingly unusual and it demonstrates just how much pressure the Government of the day was under to develop a solution to what was perceived as a breakdown in the relationship between police and public.

The 1980s of course coincided with a Conservative Government which was to remain in place throughout the decade and beyond. Interestingly, and in hindsight, the Government were clearly planning action in order to tackle what they perceived to be the excessive power of the Trades Unions. Of course, both Labour and the Conservatives had experienced considerable difficulties in dealing with strikes and union unrest during the 1970s. This culminated in the Winter of Discontent, just prior to the election of Margaret Thatcher's Tory Government in May 1979. Whatever political persuasion you, as the reader, may possess, it was clear that the Government was determined to exercise the authority of the State to resolve this situation. This was in an effort to reduce the effectiveness and disruption caused by the Unions through their continuing strike action which was a feature of the 1970s. One of the first things that the Government did was to 'befriend' the police service. They did this in a number of ways but most importantly, through massively improving the remuneration packages of all police officers. The measures put forward by Lord Edmund Davies in his report in September of 1978 to improve the financial lot of the police, was due to be implemented over a two-year period by the then-Labour Government. However, the Conservatives, on coming to power, immediately implemented the full package. Additionally, and crucially, they also brought about a situation whereby the police received above-inflation pay raises for the next few years, using a mechanism involving the official side (Police Authorities and the Home Office) and the staff side (Police Federation, Superintendents' Association and the Association of Chief Police Officers). Each year the two sides would sit down to discuss proposals put forward by the staff side. There was very little, if any, dissent, probably due to the political climate at the time. Therefore, the Tory Government could virtually guarantee the support of the police service in order to achieve its political aims in terms of wresting the power away from the Unions. This was without a doubt the most flagrant form of politicisation of the police ever witnessed. However, the majority of the British public and industry chiefs appeared to be very supportive, as the Unions had virtually brought the country to a standstill during the 1970s.

Before the real fireworks took place in the form of the 1984 Miners' Strike, the Government tried to increase financial accountability in the public sector, including the police service, through Home Office Circular 114/83. This related to 'Effectiveness, Efficiency and Economy' of State-run organisations. I recall, as an officer aspiring at this time to start to think about promotion, that this became the 'in vogue' phrase within policing circles at that time. It was regularly trotted out by senior officers and those sitting promotion boards for quite some time. However, it would be fair to say that it brought about little in the way of reformed thinking, either within policing or elsewhere for that matter. It was another thing that, in the main, was paid lip service to and, pretty much as soon as it was brought in, it seemed to descend somewhat on the scale of importance, both within the public sector as well as the Government.

# MY WAY

Therefore, the stage was set for 1984 and the Miners' Strike. The Government was riding high, relatively speaking, through the outcome of the Falklands conflict in 1982, as well as there seemingly existing a greater public feeling of contentment. The Government had, tactically and somewhat shrewdly, increased coal production to the extent where supplies were plentiful. This meant that, once they threw down the gauntlet to the Miners' Union, the latter found themselves with little or no bargaining power. Industry and domestic homes were not impacted upon and the public and industry were keen at this time for the Government to take control. Police officers from across the Country from all forces were corralled together in order to mobilise a formidable 'army'. The police response was supported by the Government through the development and implementation of legislation designed to shift the balance of power away from the Unions and towards the State. As a result of this action, the Government achieved its aim, either through design or default, of utilising the police as an arm of the State.

I do not intend here to deal with specific issues relating to police tactics and response, as this has been covered by many authors over the ensuing years. Even fairly recently, there have been calls for a public enquiry to be held, specifically to look into what became known as 'The Battle of Orgreave'. Some of the police response did not make for pretty viewing, as they were often depicted as the aggressors and in an almost militaristic context rarely witnessed by the public previously. However, the miners themselves were guilty of violence towards the police, as well as intimidation towards working miners or 'scabs', and were operating in defiance of some elements of the newly-created legislation, eg flying pickets. It would be fair to say though that the police operated with the full backing of the Government and there was considerable baiting of the miners at the time, regarding, for example, the size of police officers' pay-packets. It was certainly the case that many officers had never seen money like it before or indeed since. The vast majority were operating a week on miners' strike duty, followed by a week back in their own forces.

Even on the weeks when they were back in their own forces, they were earning overtime in order to cover for their absent colleagues. This was all funded by the Government. There were occasions where greed had a part to play and I personally know of some officers who over-extended themselves financially, on the basis of what they earned during the year of the strike, and somewhat perversely, got into financial difficulty as a result. What is not in doubt, however, is that at the conclusion of the strike, the police were viewed by some in more of a negative light than had previously been the case, especially in the minds of the working classes.

In the early 1990s, the relationship between the then still-Conservation Government and the police had changed. Margaret Thatcher had gone in 1990, and now there were a number of Tory politicians keen to change the nature of the relationship between themselves and the police service. In September of 1994, the long-awaited Sheehy Inquiry, authored by Sir Patrick Sheehy, reported its findings. This was the first, but certainly not the last, attempt by a government to 'reform' the police service. The report recommended a number of proposals which were initially implemented by the Government in full. The most far-reaching of these attempted to reduce the number of ranks within the organisation and also to 'buy out' overtime payments to the federated ranks within the service ie Constable up to and including Chief Inspector. There were a number of other proposals involving a reduction in certain allowances paid to police officers. This led to the national Police Federation kicking back and they held a demonstration, culminating in an event held in central London. The outcome of this led to the Government 'watering down' their proposals and only a small number were implemented ultimately. There would clearly be ramifications for this show of dissent on the part of the Police Federation and little did any of us know at the time what the impact on policing would be.

At this time, David Cameron was a junior minister in the Home Office. Whilst there is no evidence to support such a view, some in police circles felt that the later reforms, following a review conducted by Sir Thomas Winsor, and the stringent cuts applied to police budgets post-2010, may have been influenced to some extent by the outcomes of the Sheehy Report. As if to rub salt into the wounds, Sir Thomas Winsor was subsequently appointed to be the Chief Inspector for the HMIC (Her Majesty's Inspector of Constabulary) He was the first non-police officer to hold that post. It may also be linked to the seemingly never-ending police reform agenda that has been in existence in recent times, triggered by the Conservative Government.

Another sign of the changing face of policing has involved the numbers of police support staff employed within forces. By my retirement, Sussex Police had around 3,200 police officers supported by 2,300 civilian employees. Of course, only a fool would suggest that police officers should undertake administrative functions. Therefore, where such work is required to be undertaken, this should properly be done by non-police officers. Similarly, Human Resources-related legislation and employment law has increased manifold over the years and therefore there is a need to employ staff who are suitably qualified to work in that arena.

However, it cannot be right in my opinion that, at the height of police officer and police staff numbers within Sussex, we had around only 900 fewer police staff employees than police officers. The police service is not alone in this, to be fair. There are other public services operating similarly. A good example is the National Health Service. There are individuals working within public sector bodies whose sole job is to collect data and prepare management reports linked to this. There needs to be some radical thinking in my opinion as to whether we really need, or indeed ought to be doing, some of this? It is denuding valuable resources required on the front line. The NHS requires more doctors and nurses and less bureaucrats. The police service is exactly the same. It is police officers that are required, not support staff. Whilst such individuals probably do a good job, it cannot be right that our focus is often on bureaucratic processes and 'bean counting', rather than front line service delivery.

Legislation is without a doubt at the forefront of the need to employ a number of support staff. An excellent example is 'The Freedom of Information Act'. Whilst many may argue that this has been a good thing, designed presumably to bring about greater accountability, the Act's requirements have been responsible for creating a whole industry to support it, in every public-sector organisation. As a nation therefore, we need to seriously consider where our priorities are and indeed where they need to be. This may mean that we may have to forego some of the 'nice to haves' in favour of the 'must haves'.

One of the main occurrences of the 1990s to influence policing was the murder of Stephen Lawrence. Whilst the event itself, and the circumstances surrounding it, were tragic, the implications for the police were some of the most far-reaching ever to be seen. Clearly, once again, the matter itself has received considerable coverage elsewhere. Therefore, I only intend to highlight what I believe to have been some of the implications for the police service.

# MY WAY

One of the most thought-provoking and controversial issues raised was the view that the Metropolitan Police, and potentially the police service more broadly, were considered to be 'institutionally racist'. This is probably the best-known and widely-publicised aspect of what became known as the MacPherson Report. The reason why this caused such a furore in policing circles and elsewhere at the time is probably because readers of the report failed to understand what was meant by its author, Lord Macpherson. The term was never meant to be interpreted as meaning that the police service and its members were all racists. Rather, that there were more subtle things going on within the police service, which meant that outsiders could possibly see things as operating against some groups or individuals wishing to access its services. This had its origins in the way in which the service went about its day to day business and through some of its policies, procedures and beliefs. These could arguably be seen to disadvantage certain groups or individuals from particular backgrounds. This could of course involve a conscious or indeed a subconscious act or omission with an unintended consequence.

I attended, together several other police officers, a presentation given by ACC David Clapperton of Kent Police. He led the review into the Metropolitan Police investigation. I always remember him stating that he felt the investigation and its outcome had more to do with institutionalised incompetence rather than institutional racism. I believe that it is worthwhile considering this comment for a moment. The reason for this is that, if the outcome had more to do with a failure to investigate Stephen's murder in a professional and proper manner than anything else, then is this indicative of an organisation whose members are potentially institutionally racist? Whilst it may have been the case that there was a failure to investigate to a reasonable level, was that more about the inability of those officers employed on the investigation at the time or was there something more sinister at play? In other words, did the officers involved set out to treat this investigation in a particular way because of assumptions made, linked to the race and background of the victim? Additionally, was this as a result of the beliefs and culture embedded within the Metropolitan Police at the time? Alternatively, was this more about a poor response from an investigation perspective, made worse because of the manner in which Stephen's family and his friends were dealt with by the police?

Clearly, whatever the situation, we are left with what we are left with, and it is not for me here to question the wisdom of his Lordship or indeed the plethora of others who have written about these events. Most importantly of all, it is not for me, or anyone else for that matter, to attempt to contradict the very real views, feelings and perspectives held by Stephen's parents about the way in which they were dealt with. I raise it because I feel strongly that, regardless of the background of the victim and his or her family, as an investigator I always did my level best to gain justice for the victim's family. After all, this is all that any family has left to cling onto in terms of some kind of positive outcome. I dealt with a number of murders where the victim had a criminal history, not that Stephen did, of course. Such issues made absolutely no difference whatsoever to me in terms of the way that I dealt with it, as my own professional pride meant I wanted to achieve a positive outcome for the deceased's family. Therefore, the 1990s, similar to the 1980s before them, involved a period of considerable change for policing. This was more far-reaching than ever witnessed before. My own feelings are that, as a result of events that occurred during this time, we witnessed a change in the relationship between the public and the police, whereby accountability and expectation levels increased markedly. This has meant that it is no longer a given that the public will agree with or acquiesce to decision-making made by the police. To use a simple analogy, at the time that I first joined the service, pretty much what a police officer said or did with or to a member of the public was deemed to be unchallengeable. The complete converse is true now. Some may argue that this is for the better, whilst others may view this as a bad thing. The impact of this, however, is that the police are far more considerate in what they do and how they go about doing it. This has possibly been responsible for creating a high level of risk aversity as a result. As a society, if we are content with this as the status quo then that is fine. If not, then arguably we have only ourselves to blame.

# CHAPTER 6 – STEPPING UP TO THE EXECUTIVE LEVEL

- ❖ The new regime in Sussex – The DCI, Detective Superintendent and Chief Superintendent/DCS years.
- ❖ So, what is the difference? The changing face of policing Brighton and Hove.
- ❖ Taking responsibility operationally – murder investigation, taking charge (policing major events, eg public safety, Fat Boy Slim, demonstrations, Pride, Naked Bike Ride) and decision making. Why does it appear that some leaders in the police service joined to be something other than a 'Cop'? Is operational competence necessary in a senior leader within the police service and do they need to have worked on the 'shop floor'? The importance of 'earned respect'. The Senior Investigating Officer's role, Gold and Silver Commander. Accountability – decision logs and policy files and their importance. High profile cases. The Millie Dowler review.
- ❖ Decision making and its influences.
- ❖ Police Performance and the so called 'Performance Culture' – the risks, the benefits, inspection and accountability of police leaders. Inspection regime and getting things right.
- ❖ The influence of Chief Officers, positive and negative.
- ❖ Managing the Media or at least trying to and the pressures of being in the media spotlight!
- ❖ Partnership working and the difficulties (local authorities, magistrates etc.) of influencing them!

As a former SIO, I feel it appropriate at this point to include what is known as The Homicide Investigators Creed:

# MY WAY

*No greater honour will ever be bestowed on an officer, or a more profound duty imposed on him, than when he is entrusted with the investigation of the death of another human being.*

Ever since I first heard this, I have tried to remember every word as it should always be at the forefront of any murder detective's mind. It truly details the huge responsibility placed on the shoulders of the homicide investigator.

During the years 2000/2001, I was up to my eyes in leading major crime investigations. Additionally, I was also developing my day to day responsibilities relating to major fraud and child protection investigations, and the development of force policy regarding these areas. Inevitably, the latter involved a considerable amount of time negotiating and working with other partner agencies, including Social Services and Health. In addition, I had a responsibility to lead what were then referred to as 'Complex Case' reviews. These related to joint investigations involving top end offending in relation to sexual abuse of children and young persons, often involving multiple victims. Such investigations often involved historic cases which are indeed more difficult to secure criminal convictions from. It was recognised even then that such investigations benefited from an independent review from an experienced investigator, in order to ensure that things were on the right track. Additionally, I was involved in the review of Operation Newbridge, which was a joint police and Social Services solution to dealing with young foreign, mainly African girls, being brought into the country for the purposes of sexual exploitation and slave labour for criminal gain. Such matters have gained considerably more traction nationally in recent years and is now more commonly referred to as Modern Day Slavery.

During this period, I was also involved in leading a strand of the internal review of the fresh investigation relating to the death of Jay Abatan.

I was in my element really, especially as regards taking on the running of homicide and other serious crime investigations, as such matters have always been at the forefront of detective work and, I have always believed, provided our main reason for being there. Sussex Police was also starting to develop its future model for major crime investigation. Over the coming months, SIO colleagues Steve Dennis and John Levett and I would be heavily involved in the development of this. Indeed, Steve deserves real credit for the final outcome, as he was virtually dedicated to the task for a number of months. This involved the development of sites to contain the purpose-built major incident suites, as well as the development of the investigative structure and the recruitment of officers and staff into the allocated roles. Following the critical reviews of the investigations previously referred to, it was properly decided that Sussex needed to professionalise its whole approach to homicide investigation. It would be fair to say that we were trailing behind a number of other forces, particularly our neighbours in Kent.

Kent were very much seen as leaders in the field at the time regarding criminal investigation and also the development of an intelligence policing model, thanks to the forward thinking of their then-Chief Constable, Sir David Phillips. So it was no real surprise that the model we settled for virtually mirrored the Kent approach. In Sussex, this consisted of four sites across the county with two purpose-built investigation suites at each. In an effort to aid geography, these were located at Sussex House, Hollingdean, Brighton, Littlehampton, Horsham and Eastbourne. The facilities were fantastic, way ahead of their time, and. along with the dedicated detective resources, ensured that Sussex Police were well placed to investigate major crime in the future.

This was all happening mainly around 2001 and early 2002. It is perhaps a little ironic that what we ended up with as a model was very similar to a proposal that I put forward in my dissertation completed in 1993 entitled *Call in the Yard. A proposal for Murder investigation within Sussex Police*. Sadly, like so many things at the time, it probably got left on a shelf to gather dust! Until this point in time, all murder investigations had normally been headed up by a local senior detective, based in the area where the event had occurred. A team of detectives would then be assembled in the main from the local police division, supported by others brought in from other parts of the county. This placed a huge burden on the SIO at the earliest and most critical stage of an investigation, as the first task involved the time-consuming matter of achieving this. It often involved requesting favours from colleagues and, perhaps understandably, there could be resistance as nobody wants to willingly lose their staff. However, such a response was hardly corporate! It also meant using a room set aside in each division to be utilised as the Major Incident Room. The HOLMES team would have to come in with a transit van full of computers and spend several hours getting things set up. Again, this was extremely time-consuming and often negatively impacted on the early stages of any investigation. Due to this, the initial response was often fairly chaotic, to say the least, and definitely not conducive to assisting the priorities within the so called 'Golden Hour'. The dedicated suites and the teams to occupy these completely changed the dynamics. The staff were highly trained, skilled and professional and would immediately hit the ground running, so to speak. As an SIO, I could often anticipate upon my arrival that things would be progressing smoothly already.

One of the major developments around this type of investigation was the creation and adoption of what became known as the SIOs' Policy Book. Another way of describing these would be to name it a decision log and in fact, it is this latter title that tends to be used by Firearms and Public Order Commanders. The concept is the same in whatever format it is utilised. What happened in relation to the role of the SIO at this time was that the use of the policy book became much more formalised. As a result, training was provided within the SIO training structure, regarding its completion. The importance of the policy log cannot be underestimated. It should be the SIO's 'Bible'. Whilst reference was made to the policy book previously within national guidance, this had never really been formalised nor had it been tested through the judicial process. As far as an SIO is concerned, the policy book should almost tell a story, a chronology, from beginning to end in terms of how the investigation was run and how and why decisions were made. Some of the entries relate to administrative matters, including the investigative set up and finance etc. whilst the bulk of it is very much based on operational decision-making. I believe that, whilst actual decisions should probably command relatively short entries, the rationale for the decision could and indeed should be fairly lengthy. This should include why the decision was reached, as well as why other possible solutions were considered but ruled out. This provides the SIO with support and protection for his or her decision-making, provided the decision was a reasonable one. This is the case even if ultimately perhaps a different decision may have been a better one, taking into account the benefit of hindsight. This is particularly relevant if an SIO appears at court. I have personally experienced occasions when the defence have tested my decision-making in this way but have ultimately been told by the judge that the decision was sound, based on what information was available to me at that time. This then became what I would consider to be a considerable advance in major crime investigation.

Additionally, a separate policy book is maintained to deal with more sensitive policy decisions, including the use of particular tactics and also source-based intelligence. This can then be kept separate and dealt with appropriately and lawfully, in an effort to preserve the security of the sensitive tactics involved or indeed the individual's safety if the intelligence is source-based.

The SIO policy log or book was very quickly seized on by colleagues operating in the worlds of firearms and public order command as good practice. The system has been used to good effect in a similar manner to that of homicide SIOs, as touched on previously. The benefits are clear because there is an old adage within the legal profession which goes something like this, 'If it isn't written down, then it didn't happen'. Wise words, I would suggest, and it is hard to argue against the concept in any meaningful or sensible way.

In October 2001, James, or Jimmy, Millen, was shot dead outside his home in Tilebarn Road, St Leonards on Sea. Together with two friends, he was working on a car when a motor cycle pulled out from a turning just down the road and came towards Millen. The pillion passenger produced a handgun and fired three shots. Despite the best efforts of the ambulance service and emergency duty staff at the Conquest Hospital, Jimmy died from his injuries. My colleague John Levett was the SIO appointed to lead the investigation. While the investigation was still ongoing in late November, John and I were both attending a Linked and Serious Crime Investigation course at Wyboston, Cambridgeshire. During the course, John was taken seriously ill and was rushed to the local hospital where he was subsequently operated upon. I was tasked with taking over the Millen investigation.

Jimmy Millen was a Liverpudlian. He and his family had moved to Hastings some years previously where he had married a local woman and they had children. Jimmy had a criminal background and was well known in the area by both police and the public. So it would be fair to say that he had developed a vast array of enemies over the years. By the time I took over the inquiry, John had attempted to draw up a matrix of potential suspects. The list was very long and whatever scoring mechanism you attempted to use, it was extremely difficult to single out any particular suspects. Jimmy's criminal history consisted of wide-ranging offences from property theft, to drugs and also violence. It would be fair to say that he had few friends, more associates. I remember officers, who had conducted the house to house enquiries, recounted that comments had been made by neighbours in the area in which Jimmy lived which were of a less than helpful nature. These were to the effect that whilst they did not possess any useful information, they wouldn't give it, even if they had it. Similarly, others stated that whoever killed Millen was deserving of a medal. Therefore, as a police officer, you immediately knew that you were up against it. What I will say at this stage, however, is that those working on the investigation gave their all, in order to identify Jimmy's killer. That is a given with police officers who are professional at all times, regardless of the task in front of them. This was despite the fact that, most of the time, we were given a really hard time by members of the family, at every stage of the investigation. This included them making some very hurtful and totally unfair comments towards us regarding the fact that we were not interested in catching Jimmy's killer.

I met with the family formally every single week on a Wednesday evening together with DC Paul 'Cheesy' Hilton, the Family Liaison Officer. For the first half an hour, we had to tolerate abusive comments which included outrageous allegations of police corruption, even suggesting that we were co-operating with the offenders responsible for Jimmy's death. Having got that out of their system, we could then get down to business. As can be imagined, Wednesday evenings during this period were not a time that I looked forward to!

We had made a number of arrests of known enemies and associates of Jimmy on the lead up to Christmas 2001. None of these had led to sufficient evidence being unearthed in order to justify a charge. I had emphasised time and again to the family the importance of letting us know, warts and all, of all of Jimmy's criminal activities as these may have a bearing on what had happened to him, especially the more recent ones. During the Christmas and New Year period, I received a deputation of family members at Hastings Police Station, to be informed, albeit somewhat belatedly, that Jimmy and some of his associates had been involved in the murder of a man named Jason Martin-Smith. This was linked to a high-value burglary that they had all been involved in and for which Martin-Smith had been arrested and bailed. There was concern that he would tell the police about their involvement and therefore Jimmy, together with others, had killed Martin-Smith and buried his body somewhere unknown. To this day, the victim's body has never been located. Following the receipt of some specific intelligence, we conducted searches of a number of locations without success. Fairly recently, a man named Mark Searle, a former associate of Jimmy's, was convicted of the murder of Martin-Smith and sentenced to life imprisonment.

Sadly, and despite our very best efforts, Jimmy's killer has never been prosecuted and convicted. I still have my own suspicions as to who was involved which, for obvious legal reasons, I cannot reveal. The case still remains open therefore and I sincerely hope that, despite his background and history, Jimmy's killer is brought to justice.

Another interesting and somewhat unusual case involved the murder of the Reverend Ronald Glazebrook in Hastings. The investigation revealed that he was killed in his home by Christopher Hunnisett, a young man he had allegedly attempted to help. His body was dismembered and the various body parts were eventually found in a number of different locations across East Sussex between Hastings and Newhaven where Glazebrook had a boat moored. Inevitably, one of the lines of enquiry involved the potential for Hunnisett to have been a victim of some form of sexual abuse by the deceased. However, when he was interviewed, he never put this forward as part of his defence. He was convicted of murder and, because of his age, he was sentenced to be detained at Her Majesty's pleasure. After his release, he sought to appeal the murder conviction, having argued that his defence team had failed him at the time of his trial. He claimed that he was the victim of a sexual assault committed by Glazebrook and it was this that led him, Hunnisett, to kill him. The murder conviction was overturned and was substituted with one of manslaughter. Unfortunately, Hunnisett was later to kill another man. At his trial on that occasion, he attempted to use a defence that he had reacted to the unwanted sexual advances of the victim, Peter Bick. He maintained that he was on a mission to rid society of paedophiles. On this occasion however, his version of events was rejected, and he was found guilty of murder. He was sentenced to serve a minimum of eighteen years but was told by the trial judge that, due to the danger that he posed, he may never be released from prison.

I could of course draw on many examples of cases with which I have been involved. Indeed, I may explore this as a separate opportunity at a later stage. However, it does not fit in with the aims and objectives of this particular book. I have been involved in probably more than fifty major crime investigations over the course of my service at different ranks. The greatest accolade I have received came during my time as an SIO when, on separate occasions, colleagues have said that, if ever they had a family member who was a victim of a homicide, they would want me to lead the investigation. There can be no greater praise than that! The role of the SIO is one of the most challenging and yet satisfying undertaken by a police officer. It was certainly one of the most rewarding times of my police career.

I have used the Jimmy Millen case as an example, however, because I hope that it shows how difficult some investigations are. This is especially the case with those involving rival criminal factions. As the old saying goes, 'There is no honour amongst thieves!' It also serves to highlight the pressures, both internally and externally, placed on the SIO. Expectations are high, and nobody feels the impact of this more than the SIO and the team. I used the Hunnisett case to demonstrate how difficult on occasions the law can be to interpret. In addition, I also used it to show how, from my own first-hand experience, on some occasions the justice system, in applying the law correctly, does not always mean that the end result is the best one. This, inevitably leads to frustration, not only within police circles but also within the wider public.

During the course of the Millen investigation, Ken Jones, later to become Sir Ken Jones, took over as the Chief Constable of Sussex Police. A no-nonsense Yorkshireman, he knew exactly what he wanted and, commensurate with his birthplace, he was not afraid to say what it was and indeed what he thought! He was clearly appointed to sort things out in Sussex. Pressure had been applied by the Home Secretary David Blunkett on the Sussex Police Authority to remove Paul Whitehouse from his Chief Constable's post. He had therefore retired, and Ken Jones was appointed to replace him. In his very early days, I had been contacted by the new Chief whilst I was engaged on the

Millen case. On the day that he phoned me, he had seen me give a press interview the previous evening on the local news. He called me to tell me how well he thought I had conducted myself and the positive image it had given of Sussex Police. He arranged to come and see me and the team a couple of days later. In hindsight, I think that his visit may have had two purposes. Firstly, for him to meet team members and to get a first-hand briefing on the investigation itself. Secondly, inwardly and with the benefit of hindsight, I felt that he may have been conducting his own due diligence on me and my suitability for further promotion. I have no evidence that this was the case but, from his discussion with me, I just had a feeling that this was so.

Later-on in that year of 2002, I was approached to take a temporary promotion to Detective Superintendent. This was to set up and run what ultimately became the Crime Policy and Review Branch. This promotion was dependent upon my success at the next promotion board, as yet unscheduled. Therefore, it was a long-term period of temporary promotion. My principal responsibility was to develop an internal mechanism to review both new and ongoing major crime/homicide investigations, as well as undertaking reviews of unresolved or 'cold cases'. The best incentive I could have was that the Chief had asked for me to take up the position, as he wanted 'the best force SIO' for the position. Also, there was the fact that obviously it provided me with an excellent opportunity to prove myself in order to achieve substantive promotion.

In July 2002, I took up my posting and quickly immersed myself in it. I was able to set up what I thought was a decent response to the task, and started to undertake reviews of current investigations, reporting back to the ACC, Nigel Yeo. He chaired a meeting to look at outcomes from these as well as those involving firearms and public order incidents carried out by the force. This increased my profile within the Force and my work received considerable praise.

Sussex had, a short while previously, been asked by the then Chief Constable of Surrey, Dennis O'Connor, to undertake a review of the murder of the schoolgirl Millie Dowler. Whilst I had not initially been involved in this, I was subsequently asked to lead the work involved and then be responsible for completing the report which would ultimately go to Surrey with recommendations for them to consider. The purpose of any such review is to support the SIO and in doing this, to identify recommendations that are directly aligned to the investigation itself, others that relate to the organisation/force, and also to highlight areas of good practice. This was really good experience for me as the case was a high profile one and inevitably therefore the review attracted considerable interest.

What it highlighted to me was the highly sensitive nature that such matters will inevitably generate. The integrity of the review has to be paramount. This had been one of the major criticisms of the Stephen Lawrence investigation insofar as the reviews conducted internally initially had been fairly superficial and lacking in gravitas. At the time that any such report is presented to the SIO, or force and in this case Surrey, they are asked only to comment on the fact and emphasis contained within it. Once this has been agreed and alterations made as necessary, the report is theirs to deal with as they see fit. However, inevitably, if recommendations are not progressed or no reasonable explanation is given as to why not, then this will potentially attract criticism. There is no way that the reviewing officer should withdraw recommendations made, if they are reasonable, just because an individual or a force does not agree with them. That is the point of such a review. I would have to say that there have been somewhat tricky situations

# Kevin Moore

*In full uniform*

that I have experienced in relation to this. However, I have always stuck to what I believe to be right, regardless of any pressures. I wish to point out here that Surrey did not resist the recommendations made but initially they did seem to wish to justify in minute detail why things had led to where they were. This is perhaps understandable given the profile of the case and therefore the potential for criticism. When Jeremy Paine and I attended a formal meeting to hand over the finalised report, we did have to emphasise these issues.

As regards the world of major crime review, I was pleased to say that, along with colleagues in Kent, we in Sussex Police were seen as leaders in the field. This lead to Dave Stevens, a former Detective Superintendent from Kent, and I being asked to present at the inaugural national Major Crime Review conference in March of 2004.

# MY WAY

Before this, in March 2003, I had successfully negotiated the promotion process to Superintendent and so I had received my substantive promotion. It was a huge relief because I had been holding a temporary promotion for eight months and to have failed would have been a severe blow, both in terms of status as well as financial remuneration.

Sussex around this time, and at the direction of Ken Jones, had started out on the road of introducing a formal performance review process for divisions and departments. This involved a colleague, Chris Ambler of the Corporate Development Department, and I, together with members of our respective teams, undertaking reviews and inspections into the response of divisions to performance targets. These were set in relation to crime prevention and detection outcomes, as well as the associated processes and structures required in order to service these. This culminated in the completion of a report which would be presented by the Deputy Chief Constable, Joe Edwards, together with Chris and me, to the divisional command team with recommendations for future action. In addition, there was a fortnightly comp stat process put in place where the divisional command team would be the focus, in order to have pre-prepared questions directed at them by the Chief or Deputy related to their performance. This was in front of an audience of Chief Inspectors and above from across the force. It was a fairly daunting process for some, but it did mean that individuals in senior positions were expected to know their business. I personally have no issue with this, as I believe that this should always be the case. It goes with the territory, so to speak. At this time, there was a real emphasis on performance nationally and, quite rightly, our Chief and Deputy were determined to ensure that Sussex were not found wanting in this regard. I believe that during this period of time, we had a real focus and a healthy determination to succeed across the whole of the Force.

I was still on occasions required to undertake the SIO function in particular instances. During 2002 and 2003, I led a re-investigation into the death of Julian Webb, a man from West Sussex. His death had been the subject of a previous investigation many years previously. At the time of his death, he was married to a woman who, at the time was, known as Dena Thompson, but more notoriously later on, as 'The Black Widow'.

This case was very unusual for a number of reasons. The most significant of these for me was the fact that the case relied heavily on circumstantial evidence and the fact that there was no new evidence available that had not been present during the original inquiry, all of those years previously. What was different is that, since the death of Julian, Dena Thompson had continued to pursue a *modus operandi* whereby she formed relationships with a number of different men. She then sought to fleece them of their assets, before setting about ending the relationship through the use of violence. Richard Thompson had been the victim of a severe beating with a baseball bat which he managed to survive. Dena had convinced a jury of her innocence, claiming that what occurred was part of some kind of deviant behaviour related to their sexual relationship.

The case was also different because it involved the body of Julian Webb having to be exhumed. This in itself is a highly unusual procedure and is undertaken on the rarest of occasions. It was deemed necessary in this case as the matter involved Webb being poisoned through what we believed to be the excessive administration, over a period of time, of prescription and over-the-counter drugs.

The way in which the case was presented had much to do with the success of the subsequent conviction, obtained at the Old Bailey in December 2003, following a trial. For this, we owe a debt of gratitude to Michael Birnbaum QC, a highly skilled and eloquent barrister. Mr. Birnbaum was meticulous in the way in which he went about things, and ultimately presented the case in such a way where he invited the jury to ask themselves this very relevant question, 'What other explanation is there for the death of Julian Webb?' I very much saw this case as a victory for justice. Julian's mother had never believed that her son had died as a result of natural causes or misadventure. The result, therefore, was a testimony to her resilience maintained over a period of years. The case was later to feature as a documentary.

In January 2004, I attended one of only three Counter Terrorism SIO accreditation courses. These were brought in as a result of the burden placed on SO15 Metropolitan Police Counter-Terrorist Unit, especially in relation to terrorist activities abroad. SO15 were expected to fulfil a requirement for the UK to provide support at the SIO level, as well as provide a team of investigators. Although I was never deployed in anger so to speak, this was an interesting development from a personal perspective. For the first real time, the Security Services, MI5, were truly prepared to share highly sensitive intelligence with police investigators. This is taken as a given these days but, at that time, other than SO15, the Security Services refused point blank to discuss or to provenance sensitive intelligence in their possession.

A number of exercises, undertaken both during the course itself as well as subsequently, clearly demonstrated how valuable this new approach was. It was also my first experience of the Developed Vetted (DV) process, as we all had to be vetted to the very highest levels. Additionally, we all had to submit ourselves to various vaccinations in the event that we had to deploy abroad at short notice. It never got that far but it would probably have been just my luck to draw the short straw and get Iraq, rather than somewhere exotic like Bali!

# Kevin Moore

Also, during my time as a Detective Superintendent, I became a member of the International Homicide Investigators Association. Each year, the Association holds an annual conference for senior homicide investigators from across the world and these are normally held within the U.S. I made some very useful contacts over the years and I was also able to contribute on behalf of the U.K. This involved me arranging some inputs from British SIOs regarding relevant high-profile homicide investigations in this country. Of course, there was also an amazing social aspect to these conferences and I was able to visit venues including Las Vegas, Florida, San Francisco, Chicago and St. Louis. This was a fantastic opportunity for which I remain grateful to this day.

I met some incredible people during the course of these trips and on occasions felt terribly humble to be in the presence of some of the very best investigators from across the world. It was whilst attending the conference held in San Francisco that I first met Peter James, the crime writer. He was attending in the company of a good friend and former colleague of mine, David Gaylor. Peter's attendance at these events is mentioned as a part of the story lines involving his main character, Roy Grace. Over the next few years, I came to know Peter very well. I still attend, at his invitation, his annual book launches. I was pleased to be able to assist Peter in some way with his writing during my time at Brighton and Hove, as well as when I became the Head of the CID. Peter and I are not that close, but I still consider him to be a good friend. I have always believed that, as a serving officer, there is a need to keep relationships with those outside of the organisation, professional at all times. I know that Peter has always valued and appreciated my position. He never tried to take advantage of our relationship, but I was pleased to be able to assist him in authenticating his writing through his access to me and others. He never once got in the way and was a pleasure to work with in all honesty, and officers appreciated being able to speak to him. He has made many friends within Sussex Police as a result. Peter kindly agreed to be the guest speaker at the first CID dinner we held in 2007. For those of you who have read his books, I feature under the alias of Jack Skerrett, the Head of the CID. Prior to this, I was also referred to as the 'uncompromising and tough commander for Brighton and Hove'. He got to know me well, as you will have seen!

In March 2004, I was posted as the Superintendent Crime and Operations to the then-East Downs Division covering the policing districts of Eastbourne, Lewes and Wealden. This was the first time that I had worn a uniform since 1982! It was a real eye-opener, not least because, having been a specialist for so many years, I was now going to be managing groups of individuals with far less knowledge and experience. I was sent there in an effort to improve the performance of the division which had recently received a less than favourable HMIC inspection report. Here, I was working with Paul Pearce, the Divisional Commander, who was somebody that I knew and liked, and in the next 12 months we got on famously. A year down the line, the division had been re visited by the HMIC and received a good report this time around, with an acknowledgement of the real improvements made. I still have a copy of the report in which I am proud to say that my own part in this received specific mention.

However, this only tells a small part of the story. What the outcome demonstrated once again to me was that strong and supportive leadership from the top can really work. We had some excellent individuals working on the division at a number of levels. However, what needed to be done to bring about an improvement in performance was to corral this in an effort to make it all work towards achieving the same ends. Whilst my recent direct experience with the more general uniformed policing regime was limited, good leadership and management skills are instantly transferable. I honestly believe that what I could do was to quickly understand the main policing issues in the division, decide on strengths and weaknesses, and then, with the help of the District Commanders, put a plan of action in place on a number of fronts. This was simple and easy to understand and was very much focused on improving our response to incidents, our ability to investigate crime, and our response to general anti-social and unacceptable behaviour by youths and drunken individuals on weekend nights.

A lot of this involved developing sound systems and processes. Now I am the first to admit that I am not great on detail but there are always individuals around who are. It is a good way of ensuring that people feel involved and then buy into things as a result. Suffice it to say that I really enjoyed my time on the division and I worked with some really good District Commanders in Pete Mills, Bob Gough and Rex Matthews. Good days indeed. However, it was only to last for the year as the Chief decided that there was a job needed doing at Brighton and Hove. I was starting to become concerned by now that I was seen only as some kind of short-term Mr Fixit, as this next move would be my third Superintendent's job in three years. I was also worried that I was being overlooked for further promotion, despite turning in a performance level that was recognised in my annual Personal Development Reviews as outstanding. I was assured by the Chief that my time would come and therefore, with renewed energy in April 2005, I moved on to Brighton and Hove. In fairness, I was really looking forward to it as it was my first posting there since I first joined. However, I was to very quickly appreciate that things had changed massively since those days!

# MY WAY

My move to Brighton and Hove in April 2005, was, as it transpired, to be two years of the most challenging and yet hugely satisfying times of my career. It also coincided with my promotion to Chief Superintendent in the second year which meant I was Divisional Commander for the City of Brighton and Hove. If I had turned the clock back twenty-eight years, I would never have believed it possible then, as the most junior probationary officer in Brighton at the time, that I would later become the Divisional Commander!

I was sent to Brighton and Hove by the Chief to do a particular job. That was to sort out what he felt was the unacceptably low performance levels there at the time. It is reasonable to say that statistically at least, Brighton and Hove were in the relegation zone as far as the national performance indicators were concerned. Paul Curtis, the Divisional Commander, had done an excellent job in developing a sustainable partnership approach, working with the Local Authority. My job therefore was to sort out the more operational elements of policing. Inevitably, nobody likes to be told that the organisation or part of an organisation for which they have responsibility is failing in some way. As a result, it would be fair to say that I was not exactly welcomed with open arms. It did not help that, despite me being assured that Paul would be told in exact terms the reason for my posting, I was to discover that this was never actually done. Therefore, there were times when I felt that there may have been some resistance to my methods and my approach to bringing about change. However, if nothing else, I have a pretty thick skin and I just got on with things the best that I could. By the September, my good friend and colleague, Jeremy Paine, arrived as the Divisional Commander, which was great news from my point of view. Whilst we had different approaches to doing things, we were very like-minded in what we wanted to achieve in terms of the policing of Brighton and Hove.

# Kevin Moore

On my arrival, I attempted to set a tone. What I had noticed in my early days was what appeared to be a somewhat of a siege mentality was in existence. This was probably brought about by what some there perceived as Brighton and Hove being seen as a 'punishment' posting, where all of the difficult and troublesome officers were sent. By the end of my time there, I was pleased to be told by Adrian Rutherford, my HR Manager, that for the first time that he could remember, there were no officers seeking to transfer away from the division.

My initial view was that officers on the division did not feel sufficiently empowered to be able to 'police tough'. The good thing, from my point of view, is that there were pockets of really excellent practice. These included the Local Support Team under Inspector Andy Parr and the Divisional Intelligence Unit under DI Paul Furnell. The general CID office was also strong, containing some excellent detectives led by good Detective Inspectors. My first aim was to get all of the Inspectors on side. I knew that, if I wanted to achieve things, then this was the level that I needed to target and win the support of. Once I explained that I wanted Brighton and Hove Division to be a place that officers and staff were proud to represent, the rest became relatively easy.

I found there were many like-minded individuals who, similar to me, wanted the police to 'reclaim the streets'. I had emphasised that, while things had changed compared to my early days in Brighton, I wanted us to be respected and, to some extent, feared by the criminal elements of the city. Later on, when I was the Divisional Commander, we would introduce as our mantra, 'Proud to be Serving Brighton and Hove and Making the City a Safer Place'. This would appear on letter heads, emails and other stationary and would assist in giving a real focus for the division.

*On the front cover of the Police Review*

Graham Bartlett was Divisional DCI Crime Manager, and launched Operation Reduction around the time of my arrival. This excellent initiative was to run over a number of years and was, for policing, unusually sustainable. In its early stages, it was a police-only operation with the main focus being on an undercover/test purchase approach to the incessant illegal drug supply problem within the city. I had been horrified, on the lead up to my posting to the city, regarding the news coverage which showed very open drug dealing going on in the streets of Brighton and Hove, which was apparently going unchallenged. Needles and other drug paraphernalia were regularly deposited in public areas and some places were 'no go' areas for the general public. This was completely and utterly unacceptable. The tactics employed on Operation Reduction involved the gathering of evidence through a vast number of test purchases of mainly

Class A drugs, undertaken by undercover officers, from an identified group of suppliers. At the culmination of the evidence-gathering stage, days of action took place where the dealers were all arrested, charged and, in the main, remanded in custody pending their trial. Invariably, because of the strength of evidence against them, these individuals pleaded guilty in the main.

This was good in the short term, and following these arrest phases, the city would enjoy a few weeks of relative peace and tranquillity, with very little overt drug dealing taking place. However, shortly afterwards, enterprising dealers would fill the gap left and we would be off and running once again. It was a never-ending cycle. Therefore, we had to find a more sustainable approach. Paul Furnell and Graham Bartlett discovered that in Leeds a partnership approach had been put in place in order to target a very similar problem. This focused on not only the enforcement side as we were doing, but also on reducing the market for supply. When the action phase was triggered, they had looked to identify the drug users, and where possible, get them into rehabilitation and treatment programmes. This, by all accounts, had produced a knock-on benefit because property crime had reduced, due to the addicts committing less crime in order to fund their habits. West Yorkshire Police had been able to secure some Government funding in order to support this initiative. It is fair to say that funding is more likely if a partnership approach to problem-solving can be shown. As a result, we undertook to do similar with Brighton and Hove City Council and were successful in securing an element of Government funding. The rest is history, as the saying goes. We even appeared in the national Police Review magazine and what was achieved by all of those involved was incredible and rightly made us proud.

Alongside this, we were targeting particular types of crime, especially household burglary, putting a real emphasis on detection and locking away the perpetrators. This again culminated in huge reductions in crime, as well as improving our overall detection rates. We changed the dynamic in terms of bail. I ensured that there was a mentality where, in relation to certain types of crime ie drug supply, street robbery and burglary, there was not an automatic assumption of the right to bail. In relation to this, I sadly found it necessary to put our own house in order before concerning myself with the actions of the magistrates. Some Custody Sergeants were bailing subjects as a matter of course. Therefore, I told officers and their supervisors on the division that, where they felt that bail was not appropriate, they should challenge the Custody Sergeant. If they were met with resistance, then they were advised to contact me and I would use my powers under the Police and Criminal Evidence Act to overrule the decision to grant bail. After a few of these, I was successful in achieving my aim and from the feedback I received, I was told that the mere mention of my name to the Custody Officer worked wonders! Unsurprisingly, my decisions were never overruled by the magistrates when these defendants appeared at court because the grounds for refusing bail were totally legitimate.

Some of the reason for the support that we received from the courts was because, as a double-edged approach, I had attempted to legitimately gain the support of the magistrates. Lay magistrates are locally appointed, and one of their tasks is to reflect local issues and problems in their decision-making. I therefore felt it appropriate to ensure that the local magistrates were aware of exactly what the local priorities were. I generated a regular meeting with Juliet Smith, the Chair of the local bench. I wish to point out at this stage that the relationship was entirely professional but nonetheless, I felt that, if I was to protect the local public, then I needed to ensure that the magistrates were aware of the main issues we faced in policing. Between us, we even attempted to bring about a means by which newly appointed magistrates could go out on patrol in a police car on Friday and Saturday nights. This was in order for them to gain first-hand experience of the situations that the police faced. Whilst this was welcomed by the magistrates themselves, the Clerk to the Justices for the area was less enamoured, quoting impartiality issues etc. The good thing, however, was that the effects of the approach generally were hugely positive, and I had learned from my previous experiences that perhaps a more subtle approach could win the day! This relationship was also important in our approach to the use and implementation of the new Licensing Act 2003.

When this piece of legislation was first introduced, it was seen by many as a charter for drunkenness and general misbehaviour to prevail on our streets. While the Act did relax and extend licensing hours, at the same time it presented opportunities for enforcement and the regaining of some control over the sale of alcohol and its often negative consequences. The use of clauses contained within the legislation was to be one of our main tactics in terms of the policing of the so-called 'night time economy' in Brighton and Hove. Within a very short time of my arrival in the city, I had become sick and tired of the culture that seemed to prevail around the licensing community within the City. I sensed that there was a *laissez faire*, anything goes attitude to their responsibilities on the part of a number of pub and club owners within the city, especially in the area of West Street. This attitude was not fair on those establishments whose owners were trying to run their businesses correctly. The knock-on effect of this was an increase in violence-related offending and incidents involving serious injury. I was determined to change things through using the full powers available to us under the Licensing Act. I found some real support for positive action in Inspector Bill Whitehead, the Licensing Inspector and Andy Parr from the LST. When Jeremy arrived on the division, we decided that we would do our utmost to get on top of this issue. We policed hard on Friday and Saturday nights and supported this with high numbers of police officers through the shrewd use of overtime payments and exploitation of existing shift patterns. This also enabled us to visit large numbers of licensed premises in order to secure compliance in terms of their legal obligations. Where there were regular problems at any particular premises, then these would be specifically targeted through an action plan. Non-compliance or persistent problems could and did lead on occasions to premises being closed for 48 hours, through use of powers under the Act. This would then lead to the owner appearing before the Licensing Magistrates, where sanctions could be imposed, with remedial action being a requirement.

This really had a massively positive effect, and on occasions, even after a long day, I would work on during a Friday or an occasional Saturday, to undertake licensing visits with Andy. The effect of this was considerable. For the owners to see the Superintendent and later on, following my promotion, the Chief Superintendent in attendance, just served to enforce how seriously the police were taking things. At one time we had virtually every pub and club in West Street serving all drinks in plastic, including bottles. Individual behaviour of members of the public was also policed positively and robustly. With the extra policing presence on the streets, we got on top of bad behaviour at the very early stages, utilising the newly-available fixed penalty notices where and when appropriate.

I was extremely proud of what we all achieved in making the streets of Brighton and Hove a safer place to be. Levels of violent crime and, in particular, offences involving injury, fell dramatically. A little story highlights the success achieved. I attended a blood donation session in my home town of Seaford during this period. During a conversation with the lady taking my blood, she revealed that she and her husband lived in Brighton. She stated that recently she and he had attended the cinema on a Saturday evening. She described how much safer she felt being in the city centre at such a time than she previously had, due to the heavy policing presence. Rightly or wrongly, I took this as a public endorsement of what we were trying to achieve.

Whilst the policing side of the business in Brighton and Hove was a real positive in the main, the politics was a different story. What became apparent to me very early on were the huge sensitivities around politics with both a large and a small 'P'. Firstly, there was the local authority. Unless you have had to work with a beast like Brighton and Hove City Council, you could not even begin to understand some of the frustrations faced. Most of the time, it is fair to say that it was like walking through treacle. Trying to get anything done was a feat in itself and success, whatever that looked like, was rare indeed! On my arrival in April 2005 and throughout my time there, Alan McCarthy was the Chief Executive. He enjoyed my complete and utter professional respect. How he managed to operate in such an environment never ceased to amaze me. He was a 'local boy made good', having grown up on one of the council estates. He worked particularly well with Paul Curtis and their professional relationship was an excellent example of police and local authority partnership at its best. I would be the first to admit that such skills are not amongst my strongest! If I need something doing, and I cannot get it done because of what I perceive to be excessive inertia or bureaucracy, then I will quickly become frustrated. I recall returning to John Street Police Station on many occasions, having attended a council-led meeting, thinking how grateful I was to get back to something over which I had some control! I remember speaking to a senior council official one day and she said to me, 'Kevin, you have to remember it's not like the police where you tell people to do something and it happens immediately'. Anyone who knows me will understand the sentiment contained within this! I recall trying to get the council to consider moving a taxi rank a few yards north in West Street in an effort to make things safer. You would think that it was the most difficult thing ever undertaken. Suffice it to say it didn't happen!

One of the reasons for this problem was, of course, the fact that Brighton and Hove have rarely had a majority council, politically speaking. Therefore, it was doubly difficult trying to get anything done. I recall addressing a meeting regarding my wish to tackle head-on the problem of violence and drunkenness and its association with the night-time economy. Whilst there was some sympathy for what I had to say, the bigger issue for elected representatives seemed to be about preserving Brighton and Hove's somewhat liberal image. Even when I tried to suggest that a different approach may attract a wider and different type of clientele, thus benefitting the broader economy, it seemed to fall on deaf ears! It was like pulling teeth on occasions and far too much for a pragmatic and dyed-in-the-wool senior detective like me to cope with, in the long term!

It wasn't just the council, however, that caused me high levels of personal stress either. As I have touched on previously, I have always attempted to approach policing in a common-sense fashion, trying to envisage what the ordinary man or woman in the street would expect from their police. What I discovered very early on with Brighton in particular, and Hove to a far lesser extent, was that this yardstick is very unlikely to succeed. One of the reasons for this is that the very outspoken minority always seem to get their opinions heard above the virtually silent majority.

Whilst I respect the right of people's freedom of speech, and to be able to do what they wish to within reason, I am afraid that I do find it very difficult, if not impossible, to agree to an 'anything goes' approach to life. Therefore, I suppose it was inevitable that there would be occasions when there would be conflict between some groups or individuals and me. However, rightly or wrongly, I have always been an individual that is more inclined to run towards the fire rather than run away from it. I believe that this is what most would understand constitutes 'moral courage'.

There are a number of examples that I can draw on to highlight my involvement in situations where this moral courage as a police commander is a 'must have'. The first of these involved the policing of demonstrations in Brighton. Either as a Gold Commander in setting the policing strategy to respond to such events, or as the Silver in developing the tactical response to fit with Gold's strategy, it was my job, I felt, to respond to any adverse criticism or media publicity. I felt that it was my responsibility to draw the 'flack' away from those implementing what was put into place by either Gold or Silver. This led to me becoming public enemy number one in the eyes of certain groups and individuals viewed in many quarters as being persistently anti-establishment. My job, as I saw it, as Gold or Silver was to ensure that peaceful and lawful demonstration was allowed to take place. Despite the views of a number, in setting my policy, I always attempted to reflect this. By the same token, if groups or individuals were hell-bent on going against my attempts to uphold the law and the peace for others, then they could expect the full weight of the law to be applied. This stance included supporting local trading outlets who often faced considerable disruption to their businesses.

I could probably never have anticipated the sheer venom and vexatious nature of the responses that I received.

# MY WAY

Firstly, over the period of time that I served at Brighton and Hove as the Superintendent and Chief Superintendent, I received a number of formal complaints, requiring the involvement of the IPCC (Independent Police Complaints Commission) to conduct investigations against me. Secondly, I received any number of personal attacks through social media, some even aligning my policing style as being similar to the actions of Adolf Hitler! Indeed, a number of pictures appeared of my head and shoulders wearing a Nazi uniform. I don't look back on these occasions as me winning some kind of badge of honour but rather that I did the right thing in the circumstances. I refused to back down whatever criticism or personal attacks I might face. One quite humorous anecdote I recall involved me being filmed by the local media receiving a 'war crimes' dossier from a demonstrator, regarding the activities of EDO/MBM. They were a local company based on the Hollingdean industrial estate which manufactured a component part used in fighter aircraft. I was asked whether I would be investigating these allegations. I replied tongue in cheek that I couldn't because there were no relevant offences laid out within the Home Office Crime Counting Rules. Therefore, it did not constitute a recordable crime! Needless to say, the demonstrators failed to see the funny side of this.

The whole issue of the company mentioned previously coincided with the highly emotive issue involving the Gulf war and the UK's involvement in that. The two things were linked by those who wished to make an issue of the involvement of EDO/MBM. This action impacted considerably on policing resources over a few years as, every Wednesday, in addition to the main-line demonstrations previously mentioned, there was a demonstrative presence outside of the factory. Sometimes this consisted of a small

# Kevin Moore

*Me talking to the protestors against the EDO factory*

number of people peacefully protesting, whilst, on others, these events escalated into full-scale public order situations, needing huge police resources. There were also attacks on the premises at night and on one such occasion, £10,000-worth of damage was caused. One of the problems that we experienced from a policing point of view was that there was an apparent reluctance on the part of courts to convict those arrested for offences either linked to demonstrations themselves or to those involving the premises of EDO/MBM. One of the most bizarre of these involved a not guilty decision regarding the damage to property within the company's premises mentioned above. This decision was based on the premise that those involved did not believe their actions to be unlawful due to their having a reasonably-held belief that the damage was justifiable. These decisions in turn affected the willingness of the Crown Prosecution Service to bring charges in the first instance, using previous judgements as the basis for not prosecuting. I will leave the reader to imagine the effects that this had on officer morale, especially in cases involving assaults on police officers.

# MY WAY

I equate such sets of circumstances as being similar to operational situations faced by the SIO involved in a homicide investigation. Again, as the SIO, you are the individual in charge and therefore need to step up to the plate and take responsibility for decisions. This is particularly the case when things do not appear to be going as well as they might. It was always interesting to note those senior officers who were keen to bask in your reflective glory as an SIO when things were going well. It was even more interesting to try and find the same individuals and their proximity to me when things were not going so well! Having said this, I like to think that, in either of these cases as an operation commander or as an SIO, I never once shirked my responsibility. I am pleased to be able to say this because it is not me saying it but rather colleagues with whom I have worked in the past.

I remember also, and in particular, the matter involving the Fat Boy Slim concert which ultimately took place on 1st January 2007. During the second half of 2006 and following my appointment as the Chief Superintendent and Divisional Commander for Brighton and Hove, subtle pressure was being applied by Norman Cook, aka Fat Boy Slim and his team, to hold a follow-up beach party to the one held a few years previously. The earlier event had nearly turned into a public safety disaster and an embarrassment for the police and local authority. Whilst there were no fatalities directly linked to the event itself, this had been more as a result of good luck rather than by design. There were numerous failures which led to a potentially hugely dangerous situation. The most obvious of these was that the fact that an un-ticketed event, with no idea of numbers, was held on a tidal beach with the tide due to come in during the event itself! Need I say more?! The local authority and the police escaped by the skin of their teeth as a result.

# Kevin Moore

*Fat Boy Slim and me*

However, this had not prevented Norman and his vast array of fans seeking a re-run. Of course, I was totally against the idea. Whilst I had not been directly involved in the previous event, I had been involved in conducting some of the review work undertaken following it. Therefore, I knew full well the pitfalls and the undoubted risks involved. I was interviewed by various television channels and inevitably once again was portrayed as the bad guy adopting an 'over my dead body' approach to the issue. However, and worryingly, I had started to sense a change in philosophy from the Council. Having initially been supportive of my original stance, there now seemed to be a subtle shift, with an emphasis being placed on a potentially negotiated solution. As we all now know, this ended with an agreement to hold a ticketed event with a restriction on numbers, around 18,000. It would also be held in the winter, away from the beach and within a controlled area on Madeira Drive. I was happy to work towards this as I felt that this would hopefully serve the needs of everyone and meet the obligations of the local authority and emergency services to ensure the safety of the public as best as we could. In the event, it was cold and wet, and the greatest danger posed to attendees was potential hypothermia, which was catered for, and Norman getting electric shocks through his decks, due to the incessant rain! There was a funny story on the lead up to the event when a press conference was held. I recall Suzanne Heard, my hard-pressed Media Relations Officer, preparing me for the event. She asked me how many Fat Boy Slim hits I knew, just in case I was asked. Suffice it to say, I was in dire need of a quick lesson!

The lead up to the Pride event in the summer of 2006 was another interesting time for me. As the Gold Commander for the event, I was heavily involved with the key individuals from Pride in making the necessary arrangements. It needs to be remembered that events such as these are all about the authorities doing their best to ensure that public safety prevails. Everything was going smoothly during the course of the organisation. I had already addressed my main concerns with the organisers, regarding my wish to reduce the volume of thirteen 'near misses' linked to drugs overdoses the previous year. I had stated that it was my intention to have plain clothes police officers working in Preston Park at the main event and to have drugs dogs and officers using drug detection equipment at the entrances to the park. The organisers themselves were totally on board with this approach, as I had made the point that it was no different from the tough approach we were using with pubs and clubs where we would regularly 'sweep' the toilets in their premises for illegal drug traces. We were also on occasions using the drug detection equipment as a pre-requisite to entry to clubs with the co-operation of the management. Similarly, I had said that I would not be prepared to tolerate sexual acts occurring in a public place, again pointing out that I would not agree to such activity amongst heterosexual groups. Again, there was no dissent to the position that I took on this. However, Sue Heard became aware of rumblings in the LGBT media, suggesting that my proposed actions were disproportionate and were viewed as being seen as potentially homophobic.

Having given it some thought, I decided to ask Sue to organise a press conference the week preceding Pride and to invite all sections of the media. I recall Sue thinking that I had gone mad! She believed it to be a high-risk strategy and that, as a result, I was potentially putting myself in the firing line. I disagreed, however, and she went ahead and organised the press briefing. I had invited key members of the Pride organisers to attend also. I opened the event by outlining the need to ensure public safety prevails at any such event. I drew on the evidence of the near misses from the previous year and I emphasised that my policing style was no different to that which I employed generally on a day to day basis in Brighton and Hove. Apart from some media outlets wishing to conduct some one to one interviews following the conference, there were no questions from anyone present. I had therefore nipped any potential problems in the bud and got my points across. Sue couldn't believe how well things had gone. I merely pointed out that I felt that choosing to hold the conference was an educated gamble but was one that I was prepared to take in order to prevent the situation getting out of control. It had also served to show that we, the police, whilst supportive of the event itself, we were not prepared to jeopardise public safety or allow criminal offences to be committed.

As an aside, there were no hospital admissions for drug overdoses that year. Plain clothes officers made a number of arrests of illegal drug dealers, which was good from my point of view as it helped to justify my approach. Most importantly, the event passed peacefully and without incident and everyone was happy!

During the summer of 2006, whilst I was the Divisional Commander for Brighton and Hove, we were in the midst of a period of demonstrations which took place in relation to the Palestine situation. Much of this was seen by those taking part as justification for an anti-Israeli Government theme. The first of these events occurred one Sunday and sadly our intelligence systems had failed us for once, because we were unaware of the demonstration. An estimated group of around 400 individuals met in Adelaide Square, Hove, a well-known Jewish community area with a synagogue located nearby. They then marched to the Palace Pier where an assembly took place. Local officers did the best that they could, with the half dozen or so that could be mustered at short notice. However, it would be correct to say that considerable disruption to the general public and local businesses occurred as a result. Additionally, my officers attracted what can only be described as totally unacceptable aggression, including being spat at, and were generally abused throughout the proceedings.

The following morning, I was informed what had taken place and inevitably I was angered by what had occurred. Organisers of the event had failed to comply with legislation in place which requires them to notify the authorities of their intention to protest and the numbers involved, as well as what route they are intending to take if a procession is involved. Whilst this level of non-compliance was not unusual in my experience, the actions of those organising and then taking part in the demonstration were, to say the least, irresponsible. As already stated, the location for the initial gathering was potentially sensitive. My view was that the actions of those involved could possibly be seen by local Jewish residents as having anti-Semitist undertones. This view was later confirmed to me as being a correct one through correspondence that I received from a number of these residents.

Following the events of this particular Sunday, we received intelligence to suggest that another similar demonstration was scheduled to be held shortly afterwards. Despite our best intentions to try and identify an organiser with whom we could engage, we received no assistance in this regard whatsoever. This included a plea made through the local media for the organisers to contact us. I therefore saw this as a deliberate attempt by those involved to disobey the requirements imposed by the law.

I went ahead and organised our policing response to the proposed demonstration and this was based on the potential for around 400 protestors to take part, taking into account the previous occasion. Geoff Williams, the ACC, was to be the Gold Commander and I was the Silver. There were no real issues coming out of the event itself. A few minor arrests were made and a placard depicting the Israeli flag on one side and a Nazi swastika on the other was confiscated from a young child. This latter matter was an undoubted attempt by some involved to provoke what may have ended up being an excessive police response. However, we did not rise to the bait. The culmination of all of this was that the local *Argus* newspaper decided to run a major story of the police response, with a heavily sympathetic slant towards the protestors. I was not prepared to accept what I considered to be unjustified criticism of my officers and me. Our job as always was to facilitate lawful protest but, at the same time, to protect the rights of others and, most importantly of all, to uphold the law. Inevitably, I mentioned the origins of what had taken us all to this point ie the original demonstration, the fact that these events were unlawful and that they were also potentially seen by some as anti-Semitic. To be honest, I did not foresee the fall out that ensued. I became public enemy Number One and a number of individuals linked to this particular cause chose to make formal complaints against me, which led to me being the subject of an IPCC-supervised investigation. The outcome, however, was fairly innocuous as I only ended up receiving 'Advice'. However, as I said at the time, I would take the same course of action again if I were faced with the same or a similar set of circumstances.

Another event that caused me to be the subject of criticism involved the so called 'Naked Bike Ride'. The organisers wished for those taking part to be able to do so fully nude. As far as I was concerned, this was completely inappropriate. Therefore, I told the organisers that if there was full nudity, and officers received complaints from members of the public, then arrests would be made. Inevitably, the organisers, supported by elements of the local media, wanted to paint me as some kind of prude. However, as I pointed out at the time, this was not about me operating as the moral police. If these people chose to operate outside of the law, then my officers would respond accordingly. That was our job after all.

I have never been a 'shrinking violet' but at the same time, I have never set out to seek attention or court publicity. However, as befits my position then and at other times also, I will not shirk what I see as my responsibilities, regardless of the impact on me as an individual. I had a duty to the public and to my officers, as well as to Sussex Police as an organisation. To draw on a previously mentioned analogy, when I put myself forward for promotion, I was prepared to 'take the Queen's shilling' and therefore I needed to earn it. It was actions like those mentioned that I took then that I believe assisted me in earning the respect of those for whom

I had a management responsibility. Respect has to be earned, in my opinion. It does not come automatically just because an individual holds a rank or position. All that the latter involves is deference, which is definitely not the same as respect.

I have always felt it was right and proper to have to earn your spurs in the field. It makes life a whole lot easier if you are seen as someone who has been there and done it, rather than someone whose greatest risk involves avoiding a paper cut, sitting behind a desk all of the time! Visibility is key to strong leadership and management. I recall being told many years ago that, as a 'boss', it was important to remember the names of those who work for you and if possible, one fact about them personally or professionally. This demonstrates to the individual that you actually care about them and they are not just a number. I also think that it is a good thing to do from a personal perspective.

While at Brighton and Hove, I regularly attended briefings, just to make myself available to answer any questions raised. I also regularly walked the floors of the police stations located on the division, just to spend time talking to people, as much as anything to demonstrate that I am actually human! It helped also that, at the time, I smoked a pipe which meant that I spoke to many people standing outside like me. It was amazing how much unprompted intelligence I gleaned on such occasions!

It is probably appropriate at this stage that I cover the police and the media. I have always felt, if I am honest, that, in terms of policing, the media is almost a necessary evil. I recall attending a media-focused training course at the Police College Bramshill, Hampshire at the time that I was a Detective Inspector. It was a real eye-opener and I learned an awful lot in a week. The course organisers brought in a number of journalists and crime correspondents to test those attending, in relation to a number of different scenarios based around television and radio. It needs to be remembered that this was in the mid-1990s and there was no social media or 24-hour news coverage as there is today. We experienced live interviewing, 'down the line' interviewing and recorded interviews, and those involved really put us on the spot. By doing so, they demonstrated the need for us to be as well-prepared as possible and also that we needed to be able to think on our feet. It was good experience and assisted me greatly in the years to come. I have conducted many media interviews in my time. However, I have never been complacent as I always felt that the minute you relax or drop your guard, then there is the risk that you may come drastically unstuck.

Of course, all of the training and experience in the world cannot prepare you for the downright devious. I remember undertaking an interview with a local ITV reporter, regarding a body recovered at Beachy Head, Eastbourne, the notorious suicide spot. The deceased male was found with his wrists and ankles bound with plastic tree ties. The reporter had got to hear about this, probably from one of the numerous police sources who were the bane of mine and others' lives. I was giving my interview and I remembered clearly saying that, at that time, I was keeping an open mind as we were still investigating. I was horrified to be told later, by someone who had seen the subsequent news bulletin, that the reporter had edited in a question phrased along the lines of, 'Could we be looking at a gangland killing here?' My reply was, 'I am keeping an open mind', which was the one I gave to a completely different question. To say I was angry was an understatement. I contacted our media resources people and they in turn spoke to the station concerned. I received a far from satisfactory apology to the effect that it was a mistake on their part which occurred during the editing process. Some mistake!

# Kevin Moore

I touched on earlier a positive experience I had with a crime reporter who I will, at this point, name as being Paul Henderson. I first met Paul when he approached me regarding an investigation he was undertaking, involving homicide linked to offenders suffering from mental health problems. He wished to speak to me specifically about the case at Peacehaven involving the two young boys, drowned by their mother, covered by me earlier. During the course of meeting up with him and discussing that particular case, I happened to mention my involvement in the Daddow case. The background and intrigue involved grabbed Paul's attention. He was interested in running a feature on it. As a result, I only needed to provide him with the very basic of details, as had no wish to compromise my position. Additionally, as with any good investigative journalist, I anticipated that he would respond appropriately anyway, by going off to conduct his own investigation.

He sat through most of the very long trial and I never had any further contact with him, for fear of compromise on either of our parts. He produced an excellent article at the conclusion of the case. He protected the innocent, elderly women who had been the victims of Terry Daddow's guile through the use of pseudonyms and he depicted exactly what had happened in a most professional manner. *(See Appendix A for the full article.)* He restored my faith in journalism as a result. I wish to make it clear at this point that I received no financial reward or any other benefit, arising from my contact with Paul. I have, over the years, received payments for media work undertaken. However, this was always properly channelled into the Sussex Police Welfare fund.

The media and their approach has changed considerably over the years. Historically, reporters were ready to put in a fair amount of foot slogging to develop a story. Whilst this still happens to some extent, the effort expended, especially in relation to local journalism, has reduced radically. Arguably, what we now see is a form of lazy journalism at the more local level. Local papers have seen their circulation diminish considerably over the years with the Sussex *Argus* being a good example of this. Much greater emphasis is now placed on the sale of advertising space and also on-line news coverage and reporting. Reporters spend much of their time sitting at their desks in front of computers, rather than being out chasing a story. This has inevitably led to a breakdown in day to day relationships between the police and local reporters. There was a time when detectives knew and had the contact details of all such individuals. Nowadays, this is very rare. Some of this, of course, is probably down to the furore in recent years regarding police officers being paid by media sources for leads.

I have witnessed a significant change in the way that the police approach media releases nowadays compared to previously. It seems now to be far more structured and almost mechanistic in nature. Individual officers and spokespersons read from pre-prepared scripts virtually all of the time. I am not sure what has driven this? Maybe it is fear of saying the wrong thing or of being criticised later for something said? All I know is that, in all of the interviews that I undertook, I never once used a script. To me, such action is less than spontaneous and often, to me at least, appears to lack sincerity because the individual is not looking at the camera. Overall, I fear that it demonstrates a lack of professionalism. The officer giving the interview should know their business. Anybody can read from a script. I feel it is a sad indictment on how things have changed over the years. The drive for accountability has struck fear in the police service and it now seems that the majority are frightened of making a mistake or getting something wrong. Good preparation should always be able to overcome such concerns.

# Kevin Moore

Many have complemented me over the years for my approach to the media generally and in relation to interviews that I have undertaken. My main advice to those involved in such matters is to be honest. Also, to be prepared as best as you can and be confident. My personal experience is that there are not that many reporters out there who instil any sort of fear. Quite often, I found myself having to help them out in order to make the best of the situation, especially if I needed to get a particular message out or a particular point across. It should be remembered that they need a product from you and therefore it should be a mutually beneficial exercise. I never agreed to any interview or involvement in a documentary where there was no benefit to me as a police officer seeking information or needing to get a message across, or to Sussex Police or the police service more generally.

I had a great time and a huge number of positive experiences during the three-year period that I spent at East Downs and Brighton and Hove Divisions. It was therefore somewhat of a wrench when I received the phone call in March 2007 from Chief Constable Joe Edwards to tell me that he wanted me to take over as the Head of Sussex CID. Of course, on the one hand, it was almost my destiny, so to speak. I was a career detective and not many are able to say that they served every rank from Detective Constable up to and including Detective Chief Superintendent. On the other, I was sad to leave a place where, together with everyone there, we had achieved so much. Brighton and Hove division was held in high regard, not only within Sussex but also nationally. We were receiving numerous visits from individuals representing divisions in other forces, wishing to see and understand our approaches to a number of issues which had led to our performance improving to such a major extent. However, I was warmed by the words of the Chief. He said to me that the easy decision would have been to leave me where I was. The more difficult one was to move me somewhere else because there was an important job that needed doing there. He also mentioned that not many Chief Superintendents achieve the distinction of holding the two most challenging positions within Sussex Police. Therefore, ultimately, I did not need much convincing, if I am honest. As a result, in April 2007 I took over as the Head of CID, arguably the pinnacle of my policing career. It was probably the proudest day of my police career.

The last two and a half years of my service proved to be some of the best times, as well as some of the most rewarding. Of course, it helped that I was in the role that I guess, inwardly at least, I had always aspired to holding, certainly since I became a detective. I was keen to ensure that I made the very best of it from day one, and I can honestly say that, from my first day to my last, I had a great time doing what I believed I did best. I worked hard, together with colleagues, to really put my own specific department, as well as the wider CID, at the forefront of everything that the Force did.

Tactically, I had responsibility for everything related to serious and major crime investigation. This consisted of the areas of major crime, serious and organised crime and intelligence, child and adult protection, crime policy and major crime review and scientific support. My budget was in the region of £25 million and as always, I took very seriously indeed my responsibilities to manage this appropriately. The main difference between my budget at that point and that of my previous Divisional Commander role was that I now had greater flexibility, due to the percentages involved. As a Divisional Commander, at least 85% of the budget is immediately taken up with people and associated costs. In my new role, people accounted for around 65%, with the remainder being used in relation to processes and equipment, such as technical support and forensic science expenditure. This meant that, through my branch heads, I had a massive responsibility to ensure that the Force and my CID units were as best equipped as possible in order for us to be effective in fighting crime on all fronts. Each of my five branches was led by a Detective Superintendent or the equivalent thereof, for example in the Scientific Support Branch. Later on, I was to take lead responsibility also for the SE Regional Intelligence Unit.

I had the professional lead also for all of the force's detectives working in local police divisions. Whilst their day to day management fell to the local Divisional Commanders, I had responsibility for their professional development and direction setting, in terms of ensuring that they were operating within the priorities set at a Force level. I took my responsibilities in this regard extremely seriously. I wanted to re-instil the professional pride that existed at the time that I joined the CID. I made it my business to open and/or close every initial CID training course, as well as courses designed to enhance detective skills, in particular areas such as advanced interviewing and family liaison. I re-introduced the CID tie and neck scarf equivalent for female officers. I also organised, with considerable help and support from others, two annual CID charity dinner/dances which raised money for a number of local institutions including the Royal Alexandra Children's Hospital in Brighton and the Chestnut Tree House, West Sussex.

All of these things, I believe, helped to push the work of the CID and the detectives working within it. My arrival as the Head of the CID also coincided with a period of considerable change in terms of the policing of serious and organised crime. Together with then-ACC Jeremy Paine and other colleagues, I had to put together a number of business cases, with the aim of securing additional funding from the police authority. The purpose of this was for Sussex Police to be able to increase our capabilities as regards our response to investigating serious and organised crime. This included creating omni-competent syndicates capable of carrying out investigations, as well as being able to conduct surveillance. It included also the creation of what is known as a 'Confidential Unit' which consists of a team of officers and staff able to manage intelligence received from the most sensitive of sources. There was also a requirement to increase a number of other key posts in intelligence as well as undercover capability, in addition to enhancing our technical support. There was also to be a number of dedicated police staff posts created for the major crime team involved in disclosure and exhibit handling. The former of these has recently become highly topical again. This is due to the reported failure of a high number of criminal cases involving rape and other serious crime, where the police and the CPS have failed in their duty to disclose relevant material to the defence. We always considered dedicated support for these areas to be critical and it professionalised our approach in this area. Sadly, I understand that recent budget cuts have diminished this capability across a number of forces.

The proposal put forward amounted to funding of around £1.7 million. Even at that time, when there was less concern regarding the amount of public sector spending overall, this was a considerable increase. This was especially the case when considered as a proportion of the overall Sussex Police budget, which at that time was around £270 million. However, due the efforts of us all, including our Deputy Chief Constable Geoff Williams, we managed to secure the necessary funding. It is worth mentioning at this point, for those who do not know, that the overall police budget is made up of central government funding linked to a particular formula, and separately, local government funding obtained through council tax. This has become highly emotive in recent years as central government have made massive cuts to public sector spending, and local government have been expected to fill the gaps. I will cover more of these later when I attempt to deal with the issue of austerity and its impact on policing.

Part of my role as I saw it, as the Head of the CID, was to ensure that I maintained a high level of visibility. I had seen at first hand the positive impact of this during my time at East Downs and then Brighton and Hove. With a department, it was slightly more difficult, however, as my staff were spread far and wide. However, this did not deter me, and I racked up a lot of miles in visiting local divisional DCIs, DIs and their teams, in order to address any issues or problems with them directly. It also served to assist me in being able to secure help when I was able to, whether this be connected with funding or related to other potential barriers to progress. These regular visits seem to go down well, and I believe they assisted me greatly in being able to successfully court the support of those operating at the front end. Additionally, and probably due to my background as much as anything, I would spend a proportion of my time visiting SIOs and their teams who were undertaking ongoing murder investigations. I was keen not to get in their way, so to speak, but, at the same time, I wished to be supportive, offer advice as appropriate and also obviously maintain an oversight regarding progress. This was because these involve the most high-profile of cases. From the feedback I received over the years, I believe that I managed to achieve the correct balance. I loved this part of my job, seeing teams of individuals and trying to support them in any way that I could. Of course, as Ann will tell you, there is an impact on one's time, but this never stopped me from doing what I felt was the right thing to do. I would think that, over the years, I probably earned the equivalent of an extremely low hourly rate of pay, due to the hours that I put in. However, I never once felt that this was not time well spent. It was invaluable because it gave me the opportunity to get to know individuals and for them similarly to get to know me. I actually used to enjoy the time spent doing this and hearing about what people were working on and the successes that they had.

One example of an instance where I did get personally involved related to an investigation known as Operation Medium. This case involved a series of thirteen attacks against young women in Hastings involving violence between February 2007 and August 2008. The underlying motive was not entirely clear but the potential for serious injury, or worse still death, was clear. The investigation had been undertaken at a local level up until a point where Jeremy Paine and I discussed the case one afternoon. We correctly drew the conclusion that it was right to involve the Major Crime Branch and that they should take over the investigation. DCI Trevor Bowles was appointed as the SIO supported by DI Mike Ashcroft as his deputy. Within two weeks, they and their team had pulled together the series and had even identified a potential suspect from out of nowhere. Adam Gall, a local man in his mid-twenties, was something of a loner and an odd ball. He had barely flickered across the police radar but had come to the attention of Kent Police previously for a relatively minor matter. I was approached by Trevor as there was a reluctance by some managers for a police surveillance team to be utilised, owing to the apparent risk involved. This related to a concern expressed that, if the team could not get close enough to the suspect in order to intervene in any attack, then a victim could get seriously injured. There were potentially more conventional ways of approaching the investigation, including making an arrest at this point and relying on identification evidence from the victims. There are real weaknesses with uncorroborated identification evidence, however, and I shared Trevor's view that we should advance this to a full surveillance operation and therefore, I countermanded the decision made previously.

I am delighted that we did because, on only the second deployment, we achieved a positive result. Gall was arrested by a member of the surveillance team whilst in the early stages of an attack on another young woman. Quite rightly, everyone was delighted with the outcome. In August of 2009, Gall was found guilty of a total of nine offences. He was sentenced to serve a minimum of nine years' imprisonment but with the added sanction that his sentence was indeterminate, and he should not be released for as long as he was perceived as being a risk to society. It was the type of result that made me remember once again why it was that I wanted to be a detective.

In addition to the instances previously referred to, I regularly walked the floors of our CID HQ at Sussex House in Hollingdean. The building itself is brilliantly described in the books of Peter James and even now, I can remember the labyrinth of corridors which took a long time to work out in terms of where everything was! It consisted of an Art Deco building and, if I am honest, was totally unsuited to the purpose for which it was purchased. However, it had a uniqueness about it and it will live long in my memory. It has now, of course, been consigned to history as Sussex Police no longer have the building, and the remaining staff have moved to Lewes Headquarters.

During my time as Head of the CID, I also introduced an internal awards ceremony, soon after taking on my role. This was a regular event on police divisions, but they had never taken place previously in HQ CID. I was very keen for us to identify and to publicly celebrate our successes and praise those individuals responsible for bringing it about. I wanted to make these very formal with recipients being able to invite family members to attend, in order to share the moment with them. A buffet lunch was laid on and this seemed to add to the occasion. I arranged for Jeremy Paine as the ACC to attend and say a few words as well as our Sussex Police Authority member Carole Shaves who presented the certificates following me reading out the citations. The sceptics told me, when I first said I wished to do this, that nobody would be that interested, and attendance would be scant. However, the exact opposite was true and not once in what became a three-monthly event did any individual decline to attend in person. It was one of the best things that I ever did and went down really well.

Another success that I had early on was to replace the 24-hour scenes of crime officer coverage brought in a number of years previously. This had never been very popular and was the 'brainchild' of someone who, in my opinion, clearly did not understand the business itself and the demands placed on it. In theory, 24/7 coverage sounds good but in practice, it was never going to work unless the organisation was prepared to foot the bill in terms of resourcing it with sufficient numbers. In our situation, we were putting ourselves in a position where we were causing ourselves major difficulties, in terms of resilience, through 'spreading the jam too thinly'. This was especially the case in times such as the summer when larger numbers were taking holiday time. Inevitably, there was some pain that needed to be gone through in order to achieve what I needed, which was sixteen -hour coverage with a call out capability. We had to go through a fairly tortuous consultation process, but fortunately, the vast majority of the staff hated the 24/7 system anyway and therefore were very open to the proposed changes. We just had to ensure that we did things properly. What this example demonstrates perfectly, and hence my reason for including it, is that the police service, like so many other public sector organisations, suffers on occasions from somebody's 'good ideas'. These, in my experience, tend to be generated by individuals who feel the need to have to make their mark in some way. Generally, in policing, they tend to be those people who have no real wish to get 'bogged down' in the detail of operational policing but believe that they have a chance to excel in other areas. What is always frustrating in cases such as these is that the damage caused rarely affects them as they tend to move on to other things pretty quickly, often leaving the chaos caused behind them. This then required somebody like me and other like-minded people to come in and sort the problem out. I suppose that, over the years, I gained a bit of a reputation as a 'trouble shooter', but in all honesty, I could have done without it because, on most occasions, the problem caused was totally avoidable. This type of issue tends to happen far less in the private sector and there is a very simple reason for this. This is that often such poor decision-making has consequences, some of which involve financial loss. The amount of money wasted over the years in the public sector, and in this case within policing, must be considerable. Sadly, rarely is anyone 'brought to book' over it. There appears to be little accountability in this regard, but the damage caused to individuals who end up as victims of the poor decision-making, as well as the internal reputational damage caused, is often considerable, as well as costly financially.

During my early days as Head of the CID, it came to my attention that some lower level managers and supervisors were adopting a less that corporate approach to decisions made at the senior level. Each week, on a Monday morning, I would hold a senior management team meeting with my branch heads, or their deputies in their absence, as well as the HR and Business Managers. The purpose of these was to discuss ongoing the progress of operations and investigations, as well as any issues of a policy nature, and then additionally, once a month, to consider all human resources and finance matters. My expectation following these meetings was that any decisions made were to be cascaded down through the management structure within the individual branches. Sadly, and only in a small number of cases, I was receiving feedback that some Inspectors and Sergeants, as well as some police staff equivalents at those levels, were abrogating their responsibilities in this regard. This was manifesting itself in terms of messages being passed to the effect that, 'that lot upstairs have decided' etc. etc. I was furious when I heard about this. My philosophy has always been that, where it is possible to carry out a form of consultation, then I would endeavour to achieve this, and I would allow individuals to have their say. However, following the consultation and a decision having been made, I expected my managers and supervisors to implement these without question or any further comeback.

In order to deal with this, I felt that I needed to set a tone. I therefore arranged to hold a meeting involving every supervisor/management grade within the department, which totalled more than sixty. It was a three-line whip, with the only excuses being those away on leave or sick. Unusually for me, I prepared a script of what I wanted to say because I wanted to be sure I covered everything that I needed to. This to me was all about leadership and I wanted to make it crystal clear to all where I stood on the issue and what exactly my expectations were of them. I ran the speech past my Detective Superintendents and equivalents. One or two of the bolder ones thought that maybe I was being a little too tough. However, I was determined to do it and therefore I was going to. Unfortunately, as with a lot of things, what I was to say probably only applied to a minority. However, I felt on balance that what I was proposing to do would actually support the better managers and supervisors rather than undermine them. The room was crammed and there was not enough space for everyone to sit. However, I was standing and therefore there was no reason for others not to also. It was a Friday afternoon, deliberately selected by me because I wanted people to have the weekend period to think about the implications of what I had said, . The presentation lasted exactly fifteen minutes and at its conclusion, you could have heard a pin drop! I asked if there were any questions and there was not one. I closed the session by stating that I wished them to think carefully about what I had said and followed this by saying that I intended to attend individual branch supervisors and managers meetings in the coming month to check understanding etc. I subsequently received what I can only describe as massively positive and supportive feedback in the coming week from a number of different sources. One individual actually said that they had personally found the presentation to be 'inspirational'. Like so many things I guess that we have all done in the past, it was probably an educated gamble, but it had worked. The follow up sessions with individual branches were similarly successful and became a bit of a regular feature, with me attending their meetings on an *ad hoc* basis which provided me with a regular opportunity to test the water.

Even though it did not necessarily fit in with my main role, I put myself forward for membership of several force boards related to matters involving human resources and finance. This meant that I was able to influence a broader agenda than just the one involving my main role. This also assisted in ensuring that I was able to keep CID-related issues high on the list of priorities. Whilst this meant extra work for me, I considered it to be worthwhile in order to ensure, as best I could, the future of my department. It also meant I could influence the current and future direction of the Force. This was something I touched on previously when dealing with the period of time when I was a Detective Inspector. I always felt that I both needed and wanted this wider remit in order to be able to influence developments at a higher level.

Linked directly to this was the fact that during my time as Head of CID, I was elected as the Chair of the local branch of the Sussex Superintendents Association. I would like to think that in electing me to this position, my colleagues put their trust in me to ensure that the views and opinions of us as a group were being taken into consideration. This role was important because it applied both to the day to day running of the Force, and to ensuring the maintenance of our own terms and conditions. The Superintendents Association looks after the interests of its members within the ranks of Superintendent and Chief Superintendent. It is similar therefore to the Police Federation and the Association of Chief Police Officers (ACPO) now known as the National Police Chiefs Council (NPCC). Similar to those other organisations, it has a national body which sits above the regional boards, which for us is the SE, as well as at the Force boards. My role was a part-time one which meant that I had to fit these commitments around my day job. From this position, I was able to continue to influence events within the Force, with the added benefit of knowing that I enjoyed the support of my colleagues. I always remember Ken Jones saying to me on a previous occasion that as a chief officer, he always felt that he needed, wherever possible, to gain the support of the Superintendents and Chief Superintendents as this made his job an awful lot easier. He didn't phrase it quite like that but that was the sentiment contained within what he said!

One of my responsibilities, together with the branch secretary, was to meet regularly with the Chief in order to discuss any issues affecting our members. I always found Martin Richards, the Chief Constable, to be very receptive and approachable in this regard and very amenable. This highlights the benefit of dealing with chief officers who themselves have performed at other levels within the organisation, as they have a good understanding of the issues. In fact, there was probably only one occasion when I came close to falling out with the Chief. This involved a review that was being undertaken of human resources and finance provision within the force. Up until this point. 2008/2009, we'd had a mixed response with provision of both at the local and Force level. This had served us well up to this point but my colleagues and I recognised that there was a need to consider how efficiencies could be made, if at all possible. I recall in the early stages speaking to the HR Director, police staff equivalent of an ACC, that I would welcome full consultation as regards both my colleagues and me. Far from this happening, unbeknown to us all, the HR Branch met in isolation and drew up a proposal for the future with no prior consultation with the staff associations. I found out about this on a Saturday morning whilst I was attending a national Superintendents Association meeting in Woburn. I received a phone call from a trusted HR source who told me what had taken place the previous day. I was livid. I immediately phoned Jeremy Paine, expressing my concern. He, like me, knew absolutely nothing about it but promised that he would make some enquiries.

The outcome of this was that a meeting was arranged between the Chief Superintendents, ACC Robin Merrett and the HR Director. I felt sorry for Robin because he was placed in a really difficult position, trying to defend the indefensible. There was no real outcome and we were informed that the proposal was due to be tabled at the Force Policy Board meeting scheduled for the following week. Of course, I was ready to go into battle and, after the paper had been talked through by the HR Director, I let rip! I made the point that there had been no consultation over what was being proposed which was to re-centralise all HR resources, a hugely retrograde step in the opinion of my colleagues and me. I stated that I could not see where any savings were going to come from, to which the response was that that was not the priority at this time. This served only to make me even angrier. What she appeared to be proposing was a fully-centralised model, which effectively amounted to empire building, with no obvious benefits and no savings anticipated. Suffice it to say, I lost the argument but that was not the end of the story.

The following day my PA, Julie Bishop, received a phone call from the Chief's PA. He was due to attend Sussex House the following afternoon to sign some surveillance authorities requiring sanction at his level. He wished to see me following this, even though Julie had explained that I was chairing a meeting of the Major Crime Review Group. It was clear, however, that I was expected to withdraw from this meeting in order to see the Chief. This duly occurred the following afternoon. What took place was somewhat bizarre, from my perspective. I was expecting a rollicking, to be honest, for what had taken place at the Force Policy Board. What happened instead was that I was asked if everything was all right, because he felt that I was becoming very angry of late. I explained that I was absolutely fine but if he was referring to what had taken place at the meeting, then yes, I was very angry about what had been proposed. However, most importantly of all, I was angry about the process leading up to the decision being made and the total lack of consultation. The Chief pointed out that my approach had upset the HR Director. I countered by saying that, while I was sorry that this was the case, I would not be apologising because I felt I was well within my rights, both as a departmental head but more importantly as chair of the local Superintendents Association. I appreciated, following this, that I had probably received some kind of reprimand, but if I had, it was not very clear. If I had received one from Ken Jones, then I would have been left in no doubt that this was the case! Fortunately, I never received one from him!

I think one of the things that this made me appreciate was that probably my days were numbered. I was about to enter my thirty first year of policing and at that time, thirty years was the point at which an individual could draw their full pension. Whilst I loved my job, I was in a position where I needed to consider my future. Jeremy was due to retire in March 2009 after completing his thirty years and I was therefore aware that my 'top cover' would then be non-existent. None of the previous chief officers who had supported me were any longer in post. I had been extremely grateful for the support that Jeremy had given me over the years and I was not convinced that whoever his successor was would be prepared to do similar. The old saying of 'if you live by the sword, you have to be prepared to die by it' was once again relevant at this point in time, I felt.

Things were also starting to change in a number of other ways. We were about to embark on a period of time where massive savings were going to need to be made in policing, as well as the wider public sector. The financial crash had taken place in 2008 and everyone was starting to feel the pinch. Frankly, I did not have the stomach to see all that I had witnessed being built up, in terms of the development of a response to the policing of major and serious and organised crime, pulled apart. Also, there were financial considerations at a personal level. Every day worked from this point onwards meant that I was continuing to contribute to a pension that was already paid for. Additionally, there were also rumblings that Sussex were going to follow the lead of other forces and implement what is known as Regulation A19 under the Police Regulations. This gives the power to Chief Constables and Police Authorities to effectively force through police officer retirements at the thirty-year mark for efficiency purposes. For this, read cost savings. This was ultimately implemented in 2010 after I had retired.

It was with a somewhat heavy heart that I decided to give notice of my intention to retire in September 2009 after what would be a total of thirty-one years and three months.

There was still one major event for me to look forward to, however. Through the Superintendents Association, I had been nominated to attend one of the three annual Buckingham Palace Garden Parties in July 2009, together with Ann. I had met the Queen during my time as the Divisional Commander for Brighton and Hove in early 2007, when she and Prince Philip had attended Brighton to open a number of venues within the City. I had attended a lunch event at the Brighton Racecourse, together with the Chief Constable Joe Edwards. I am a staunch Royalist and the invitation to Buckingham Palace was indeed something to look forward to. Sadly, the day was ruined to some extent as, virtually immediately after the Queen had conducted her 'walk about', the heavens opened and there was a massive thunderstorm, flooding the local area including Victoria Railway Station. Ann's best frock was soaked through and ruined, as was my all wool-suit which shrunk! However, I will never forget the event and the privilege afforded me through my invitation to attend.

Having put in notice of my intention to retire, I had a few months' grace, in theory at least, in order to decide what I wanted to do following retirement. Ann and I had obviously discussed the future in some depth. When a police officer retires, in terms of their pension, there is an option to commute some of this in order to receive a tax-free lump sum, together with a residual pension. The police pension is a good one. However, we pay a considerable contribution towards this and therefore I resent it when people outside the organisation try to equate it with some kind of 'golden handshake'. Also. Police officers work hard in the main throughout their careers. Their salaries are not huge when compared to some working elsewhere and who probably do not have the same level of responsibility. Ann had by choice stopped working in 2007 on the approach to our daughter Kelly's wedding which she was busy organising. Having worked for more than thirty-one years, I did not wish to use the majority of my lump sum pension payment to pay off our mortgage. By the same token, I did not want a job that meant that I had to continue working quite as hard as I had been, especially following my various promotions. This was one of the reasons that I did not wish to take the IPCC position that I have previously referred to.

In the end, I loved policing and therefore, it made sense to find a job where I could remain working within the police but in a less responsible role. Initially, I was successful in securing a position within Sussex Police as a major crime review officer. This was a role in which I would be able to draw on my experiences of homicide investigation, as well as my previous involvement with undertaking reviews of ongoing murder investigations and unresolved or 'Cold Cases'. However, as I was working up to retirement, I was offered an opportunity to work, in the short term to start with, as the Intelligence Manager within the fairly recently-formed SE Regional Intelligence Unit. This was later to evolve into the SE Regional Organised Crime Unit. I had the inbuilt safeguard of knowing that, until this role was formally advertised, the position to which I was due to go to would be held open for me. This was pending my decision as to whether to apply for it in the longer term and whether I was successful in securing it, if I did.

# MY WAY

My last day as a serving police officer was inevitably one filled with a whole plethora of mixed emotions. I remember driving to Sussex House on my last day and thinking to myself that this is the last time that I would be undertaking that journey. I was in many ways sad because I loved my job and, unlike some approaching retirement as a police officer, I had no regrets, only happy memories in the main. At the same time, I acknowledged and accepted that all good things do have to come to an end. I had achieved so much in terms of my own career and felt justifiably proud of this. I also had an abundance of stories to recall and recount, and I left with a string of compliments ringing in my ears from colleagues past and present. It was time for me to move on with my life.

At that point in time, little did I know what awaited me when I started in my new position on 21st September 2009. Far from it being a quieter and less taxing role, it was to prove to be one of the most challenging periods of my career in policing.

# CHAPTER 7 – THE REGIONAL AND THE NATIONAL

- ❖ Traditions – RCS, NCS, NCIS.
- ❖ How does it work? – Local, regional, national.
- ❖ Does it work?!
- ❖ Outside pressures and influences – forces, PCCs and Governmental.
- ❖ The politics of regional working.

Regional and national working is not a new phenomenon in policing or law enforcement in its widest sense. The Regional Crime Squads or RCS go back many years. The response, similar to more modern times, was geared towards targeting top level criminals whose activities crossed traditional force boundaries. Their criminality meant that it was difficult to deal with them, as forces simply did not have the resources or the expertise to handle the individuals involved.

Television fiction started helping the public understand the type of criminality involved when *Softly, Softly Task Force* hit our screens, with Stratford Johns portraying DCS Charles Barlow and Frank Windsor playing DCI John Watt. The programme was very popular in the late 1960s and whilst it was fiction, it did provide an insight into the workings of the Regional Crime Squads.

There were nine regions in total, with the South East known as the No.9 Region. Such teams would work either as individual units within their own regions or come together with colleagues from other areas, as and when the need arose. They had their own command structure but were funded by the forces within whose region they operated. This meant that there was always, in theory at least, a line of accountability. The main criticism, however, was that the RCS worked in isolation to forces, with very little connectivity between the entities. This would often lead to conflict with so called 'Blue on Blue' situations arising, which could potentially compromise police operations and investigations. The Crime Squads were in effect 'stand-alone' bodies, possessing their own surveillance and armed capability, as and when required. The detectives working within them were omni-competent and therefore these units were pretty much self-sufficient. This to some extent compounded the views of some that they were a law unto themselves with little accountability being evident.

As we entered the 1990s, the regional crime squads were distanced even further from forces with the advent of the National Crime Squad (NCS), as well as the National Criminal Intelligence Service (NCIS). The drive with this model was that whilst the NCS would still have regional offices and teams, the emphasis was to operate at a national level and deal with national priorities. The operating model involved the NCIS developing the necessary intelligence packages for the NCS to feed off and their focus was to target the most serious and organised criminals, whose groups operated across the whole of the country.

Arguably, the model concerned was pretty effective and there were a large number of celebrated successes. However, as with many things, politics plays its part whether this be in the form of traditional party politics, or whether it involved internal police politics and the latest group of the dreaded 'ideas' people.

The culmination of this led to the birth of SOCA, the Serious and Organised Crime Agency. Whatever your politics, this ultimately proved to be a failure. Whilst certain of SOCA's responsibilities, such as dealing with instances of kidnap, continued to be provided professionally at that level, the main focus of targeting serious and organised crime was less effective. This was for a number of reasons arguably. Firstly, the recruitment to SOCA was a disaster in many respects. The hope was that the majority of the police officers who formed the NCS would move across to SOCA. However, this was not the case because, in addition to recruiting police officers, they also took on staff from HM Customs and Immigration, and therefore the terms and conditions of employment were fundamentally altered. This meant that police officer pensions were potentially affected, and a number of other existing benefits were also removed.

There was also conflict and mistrust between the different agencies making up SOCA. This, to some extent, was inevitable and should have been foreseen by those wishing to progress this model. This problem continued throughout the existence of SOCA and was never overcome. The impact on investigations and operations was considerable and was worse in some areas than in others. There were some good and highly professional operatives working within SOCA. However, in the main, they just did not fit together as well as had been envisaged. Another potential reason for the failure of SOCA was that they were targeting the national and international, with little or no involvement at the regional and local levels. This also inevitably meant that the vast majority of their time was spent dealing with the importation and illegal supply of Class A and B drugs. This is not in itself a bad thing because, as any police officer would agree, there is an inextricable link between drugs and other forms of organised crime. However, the whole thrust of SOCA's activity was at the front end of importation and supply of commodity. There was huge criticism, therefore, that the gap was widening between the international elements of organised crime and the national, regional and local. Therefore, the Regional Crime Squads had never truly been replaced.

This situation then led on to where we are now with the advent of the NCA or National Crime Agency. Arguably, this is just a variation of a theme with a different title and different structure. It has brought together more law enforcement agencies under the NCA umbrella than existed with SOCA. The operating model is very similar, however, with regional offices still in place but with a centralised emphasis now with a number of functions, such as Child Exploitation on Line, being dealt with via a national hub.

Probably the most fundamental shift in emphasis to have taken place is the development of a clearer structure as regards the local, the regional and the national. Whilst SOCA was being developed, an agenda had been commenced to look at plugging the gap caused through the demise of the former Regional Crime Squads.

This involved the creation of what are now known as the ROCUs or Regional Organised Crime Units. Nobody wants to call them Regional Crime Squads for fear of criticism of having done away with them in the first place! The development of these teams has been extremely painful, to say the least. The main reason for this, of course, involves funding. Bearing in mind that the bulk of the time when ROCUs have been developed has fallen during a period of austerity, this has clearly had a major impact.

Having removed the Regional Crime Squads in their entirety, there was then a need to demonstrate time and time again to chief officers, Government officials and numerous others that there was now a need to recreate something which had previously been dispensed with. Part of this, of course, inevitably involves having to deal with both fragile and inflated egos, as well as encouraging chief officers to hand over funding, officers and staff. This is far from easy. The problem is then compounded by a lack of willingness on the part of successive Home Offices and Governments to actually set a clear direction.

Even the element of funding provided by the Government has been a fudge. Ever since the advent of the

ROCUs from the mid-2000s, there has been no permanent funding provision. This has always been undertaken on a year to year basis, hardly a recipe for a smooth passage or conducive to convincing officers and staff to apply for positions within the set up. When considering this problem, comparison also needs to be made with the response to Counter-Terrorist policing in the UK and its funding, compared to that of Serious and Organised Crime investigation. There is actually no comparison to be made, realistically speaking! I think that the vast majority of individuals, including myself, would have no problem with the levels of funding supplied to such a critical area as counter-terrorism. However, by comparison, the funding of serious and organised crime investigation is very definitely the poor relation. Therefore, it is not difficult to see why the latter has taken much longer to get off the ground and to be able to demonstrate its value.

In the South East region, we have also experienced the complication of dealing with one of our forces, Kent. We never knew whether they were part of our set up or not. Again, the Home Office has refused to intervene in order to provide clarity of direction. This latter issue has its history in the days some years ago when force amalgamations were on the Government agenda. A number of the larger provincial forces, Kent being one of these, argued that they were a large enough enterprise to be able to stand alone in a strategic sense. Kent's position then changed slightly when they decided to pursue a working partnership with Essex Police as, in their view, this lessened the need for a regional approach. This was even though the River Thames separates the two counties who have very little in common, it has to be said.

The development of the ROCUs has been somewhat piecemeal. The East Midlands have always been seen as the front runners, thanks to the Chief Constable of Derbyshire at the time, Mick Creedon. He had the presence of mind and the foresight in the mid-2000s to see how things were likely to develop, as regards the future investigation of serious and organised crime. He was able to secure Home Office funding to support regional development in that area. Additionally, and critically, he was also able to win over his colleagues in the other forces in his region through championing the cause. This is something that we were never able to achieve in the SE Region as there was never a Chief Constable who either felt able to or indeed had the will to corral their colleagues, in this regard. Therefore, we were always going to be on the back foot. The end result of all of this has been that the ten ROCUs across the country have all been at different stages of development and this is still the case even today. This has inevitably led to an inconsistent approach.

In terms of the SE, as with some other regions, it has to be said, we only got ourselves up and running in April 2007 with the creation of the SE Regional Intelligence Unit (RIU). At that time, the Unit itself was not even truly viable as an intelligence unit. This was because it did not have all of the posts filled that would have led to it being more effective in terms of what it was meant to achieve. Forces were reluctant to second officers or staff to the unit and there was a general reluctance to support the concept of a regional intelligence unit in any meaningful way. At the time of its inception, Sussex Police had the regional lead for counter-terrorism which had its roots in the period of time that Sir Ken Jones was the ACPO (now NPCC) counter-terrorism lead. This meant, in terms of a default position, that the RIU was aligned to the existing SE CTU (Counter-Terrorism Unit) in terms of its day to day line management. This was because nobody had really considered, at the time of its inception, whether or not this was appropriate. The Unit itself was run by an Intelligence Manager, a role which I was later to take on. This situation continued to exist until early on in 2009 when Sussex relinquished the CT lead to Thames Valley Police. Following a discussion I had with Jeremy Paine, Sussex made a bid to take the lead for the SE RIU., not that we had to fight anyone for it! However, it seemed the right thing to do as it was housed in Crawley, West Sussex. This led to joint funding being found to appoint a Detective Superintendent to lead the Unit. Once this appointment was made, things started to move forward in a positive sense, as small amounts of additional funding were begrudgingly handed over by the forces of the SE Region. This was just enough to ensure a viable SE RIU through the creation of and the recruitment to the relevant posts.

In July 2009, just two months away from my retirement, I was approached to fill the Intelligence Manager's position which had at that point become vacant. My post was the police staff equivalent of Inspector/Chief Inspector. The salary was reasonable for the role but certainly not excessive and I was to give what I thought was full value for the money over the next eight years and four months! At this time, Sussex Police still had a regional lead responsibility for the RIU and later what was to become the ROCU.

When I started in September, the priority set me was to ensure that we were in a position to 'put up' at least one intelligence package for consideration as an investigation at the next SE Regional TTCG (Tactical Tasking and Coordination Group) meeting. As it turned out, we did better than that and came to the table with two potential investigations. However, of course, we had no investigative or operational arm to tackle such investigations. This meant that, if an investigation were adopted, then a 'task force' would need to be created to deal with it, together with the appointment of an SIO. This is easier said than done and, having been challenged to prove the worth of the RIU, we had in fact now become a bit of a nuisance, if the truth were to be told. This was because now there would be a need to develop a response. I remember vividly the day of the meeting in question. When we were looking for a lead force for the two investigations, you could almost see heads disappearing behind the table top! Eventually, leads were agreed for the two investigations and then the real fun began. I was tasked with pulling together the resources to mount two regional investigations. This was not easy, as geography played a significant part. After considerable pain and anguish, we managed to put in place a suitable response for both the investigations. One of these involved a group of criminals undertaking industrial-scale cannabis cultivation on a national level, using Vietnamese 'gardeners' who were often illegally trafficked into the country. The other case involved the theft of plant valued at £100,000s. Both cases were ultimately dealt with by the respective SIOs appointed to deal with them, with varying degrees of success.

These were followed by another investigation developed by us relating to a national series of robberies and thefts of cigarettes and tobacco goods from Palmer and Harvey lorries across the country. The MO *(Modus Operandi)* involved the identified suspects sitting near distribution depots and then intercepting the lorries and their drivers at the point of their first deliveries when most of the goods were still on board. Initially, due to the national reach of the offending, I attempted to have the case adopted as a nationally-led investigation through the national RIU managers forum. This bid was unsuccessful and culminated in what can only be described as an attempt at disrupting the criminal activity involved, which was negotiated to be handled by Kent Police. A less than satisfactory conclusion resulted, and whilst arrests were made, no charges ensued. However, following a number of complaints made by officials from Palmer and Harvey, relating to a continuing series of offences committed in the London area, the

Metropolitan Police made some arrests leading to prosecutions. This successfully disrupted the offending in the short term. However, it is fair to say that such criminality continued over the next couple of years, instigated by an extended well-known criminal family, domiciled across the whole country. Palmer and Harvey had in excess of sixty distribution outlets nationally and therefore the MO used was easily transferable by those involved. Several million pounds' worth of goods were stolen over a two-year period. Relatively few arrests and prosecutions arose as a result. However, this example served two purposes at least. Firstly, it highlighted, if it needed to be, the complexity involved in cross-border crime at a regional and national level. It also highlighted to senior officers in the SE Region and elsewhere that RIUs needed to have their own operational and investigative capability, instead of relying on forces for this.

At a national level, funding was provided to create a regional response to deal with money laundering and financial asset confiscation from those involved in the commission of serious and organised crime. As regards ourselves in the SE Region, it was also agreed to fund, from force budgets, investigative resources capable of conducting surveillance operations. As mentioned previously, this was in 2010 at a time when forces were really starting to feel the financial pinch of austerity policies imposed by central government. Therefore, whilst we ended up with a response of sorts, by their own acknowledgement the force representatives agreed that the numbers involved were only half of what we really needed as a basis for operating at this level. The officers and staff recruited were meant to either already be or prepared to be, omni-competent in terms of investigative and surveillance skills. This was only the case with a small number, and therefore we had a lot of individuals who were surveillance-accredited only or solely detective investigators. This clearly had an impact on the overall effectiveness of the ROCU, as we were soon to be known as. The balance was skewed and therefore either we were putting in excessive effort in terms of surveillance-related responses or, alternatively, we just did not have enough investigators to go around.

This was definitely not a good place to be in and inevitably we were often in one of two places. Either we had too many intelligence development cases ready to move to the investigation phase, with scant numbers of investigative officers to respond. The alternative situation meant that the investigations syndicates, and ourselves in intelligence development, were vying for the same surveillance capability. It would be fair to say that this brought about considerable internal strife and conflict. Coupled together with this, levels of expectation on the part of our constituent forces were excessive. We found ourselves bound up with large amounts of bureaucracy designed by others, to ensure that we were always accountable. Performance tables and reports were constantly being prepared and tabled at various meetings, many of which were never even acknowledged, let alone acted upon. This also mitigated against us in terms of what we were able to deliver. Looking back with the benefit of hindsight, I don't believe that I would ever have taken on the role if I had known what I would face. What with internal as well as external politics, I and others were suffering. Trivial internal issues were starting to become the norm. I found myself having to justify my position to line managers above me who frankly did not, in my view, understand the situation that we were in. The focus seemed to me to be on attempts to undermine the efforts of individuals and I increasingly once again found myself having to support those being treated unfairly.

One such instance involved a detective sergeant working for me who had recently been promoted into the role. As part of his promotion procedure, he had to maintain a work-based assessment which I needed to sign off, in addition to an overseeing local Sussex Police Training and Development Inspector. I was approached by this inspector who told me my line manager had tried to block the signing off of the work-based assessment. He was saying he did not agree that it had been satisfactorily completed, despite the inspector and I providing evidence to show that it had. Together with the Head of Unit, they had determined that the Sergeant concerned should return to force in order to enhance his own development opportunities. I asked what evidence they were producing to justify this course of action and of course they couldn't provide any. I was also accused of being too close to the individual which I was able to show was simply not the case. The Training and Development Inspector was so concerned as to what had taken place that he formally reported the occurrence in writing to his own line manager. The outcome was that my stance on the issue was supported and the sergeant concerned remained in his position. While I felt fully vindicated as a result, once again it did nothing for me in terms of how I was viewed by some!

I always felt during my time with the SE ROCU that senior managers within the Unit were finding the levels of accountability and scrutiny, as well as the doubting of the concept itself, difficult to cope with. This led to them focusing on tactical details, rather than the more strategic areas of their responsibility, meaning that we were almost seemingly turning in on ourselves. Many of us at the operational level were finding this difficult and morale was low. A number of officers and staff were voting with their feet and returning to their respective forces. This issue was to escalate still further in the years to come. I suppose inevitably once again these events did not make me very popular with managers above me. However, I still felt that, in cases such as the one that I have described, the right thing to do then was, and always will be, to support those being wronged.

I became ill during the first half of 2011. The constant battles with senior officers in our forces to justify our role and even our existence, together with the seemingly never-ending sniping and politicking at a local level, took its toll on me. I had never felt this way before in the whole of my working life. I wasn't sleeping very well and, unusually for me, I was feeling quite lethargic. I had become almost paranoid, believing that any errors on my part, or those of my staff, would result in them or me being the subject of some kind of targeted activity. I had already experienced a hugely negative PDR annual review process the previous year. During this, my line manager seemed to have trawled deliberately to pick up on the slightest things that he could use to undermine me and my position. I was feeling that, because of my background and experience, I was perceived to be some kind of threat to senior managers, although not for the first time admittedly. It culminated in me seeing my doctor who diagnosed me as suffering from anxiety. Whilst I was prescribed medication to assist me, I am pleased to say that I did not take any sick leave. I felt inwardly that if I did take time off, going back would prove to be harder than if I continued as I was.

Eventually, things settled down to some extent. It has never ceased to surprise me that, in some cases when individuals have somebody working for them who possesses a particular skill or ability, they do not feel able or want to exploit this in a positive way. I always sought to use such attributes to my advantage. However, as the years have gone by, I see this happening less and less now as regards those holding senior positions.

One of the major problems that we had within this region was the fact that we did not have a chief officer lead as such.

For example, in the East Midlands, they had DCC, now Chief Constable, Peter Goodman. He had worked closely with Mick Creedon and the national lead for serious and organised crime, Sir John Murphy, latterly the Chief Constable of Merseyside. These individuals were 'big hitters' in this world and we would have benefitted greatly from somebody at a similar level to support us. The fact that we didn't has consistently meant that, over the years, we have found ourselves vulnerable to the whims of individual chiefs and other senior officers. This has inevitably impacted on those senior managers operating within the SE ROCU who have often been isolated from any real or meaningful senior support. As a result, they have had my full sympathy in that respect. I acknowledge the fact that this has placed them under unnecessary pressure which has impacted on them individually and the ROCU more generally.

I had a great team of officers and staff working across the intelligence unit, performing a number of different roles. They were highly productive and put together a large number of very different intelligence packages, aimed at tackling a wide range of organised crime groups (OCGs). I have already touched on some of them. However, others included Operation Farmer, which successfully targeted a group of London-based criminals committing robberies against banks and building societies in the South of England.

We also put together and co-ordinated a national response to burglaries committed by Columbian-born criminals using false Mexican visas, targeting Asian homes where rare, high carat gold was the commodity stolen. We also successfully targeted a group involved in the large-scale importation of major quantities of a pharmaceutical cutting agent used with Class A drug supply.

Operation Holdcroft was a response we put together, targeting the problem which has become widely known as

'County Lines'. This involves members of London gangs taking over the 'turf' in the Home Counties and elsewhere across the country, in order to supply Class A drugs. The term *County Lines* relates to the mobile phone network utilised for this purpose. Op Holdcroft was the forerunner to a much broader national initiative and was recognised at Home Office level to be the very best of practice. We organised the holding of a regular quarterly forum which, while mainly for the benefits of the Metropolitan Police's Op Trident and the SE Region, was attended by many other forces and regions, including Scotland where County Lines impacted also. We were also seen as leaders in the field of human trafficking and organised immigration crime.

There were many other similar instances, but these examples give a flavour of what was achieved. I feel justifiably proud of my team's successes and the individual members who formed it. They were a credit to themselves as individuals as well as the SE ROCU and the wider response to the targeting of Serious and Organised Crime.

The next couple of years were a lot better and the new Head of Unit was a lot more confident in his own ability and sure of himself. He appeared altogether less sensitive, within reason, as to how senior members of constituent forces viewed us in the SE ROCU. This meant that there was much more of a 'take it or leave it' approach, which seemed to reduce the pressure felt by everyone within the SE ROCU. I recall this individual once describing to somebody that he viewed me as being something of an enigma. Apparently, there were times when he saw me in a more critical light, due to my somewhat robust approach to things, and others when the opposite was true. This followed on from him receiving some positive feedback about me from a senior member of another agency. He also once told me that someone had described me as being 'constructively belligerent'. In the context in which these were used, it appeared that they were highly positive comments as they arose from contributions that I had made whilst attending national meetings. I make this point here because, whilst I accept that my style and approach may have appeared to some to be challenging or even potentially aggressive, this does not mean that I was wrong. I accept that some may have found me difficult to deal with as my manager but nonetheless, my priority was always the organisation and my staff. Therefore, if my response upset them as individuals, then so be it. However, I make no apology for this because I felt that at all times it was the right thing to do.

The next stage saw ROCUs developing a greater capacity nationally, brought about through Government funding which had to be matched by forces. This brought about the implementation within every ROCU of what became known as the 'Twelve Creedon Core Capabilities', named after CC Mick Creedon. The capabilities involved were intelligence, prison intelligence, fraud investigation, money laundering and asset confiscation, confidential unit, cyber-crime response, investigation and surveillance, operational security, GAIN (Government Agency Intelligence Network), technical support, covert operations and undercover policing and witness protection/protected persons. The SE ROCU was one of the first Units to secure all of these capabilities. However, our total resources were small in comparison to most others. Total staffing numbers were only just over 200 altogether. I make this point because, in considering the level of resources that we had available, one needs to take into account the size of our region, which is significant. The SE takes in the force areas of Thames Valley, Hampshire, Sussex, Surrey and Kent. Other similar-sized regions, such as the South West and Eastern, were boasting at least half as many resources again.

# MY WAY

1st April 2014 was to be something of a red-letter day for the SE ROCU. It was on this date that Thames Valley Police took lead responsibility for the Unit, the idea being that we were to have a joint command consisting of the SE CTU (Counter Terrorist Unit) and the SE ROCU. This would mean, for the first time, that we had an ACC lead. The model of operation for the CTU was a 'host force' one, where officers and staff, rather than being seconded to the Unit, were actually expected to resign from their existing force and join Thames Valley Police. Whilst this did not significantly alter basic terms and conditions, it was not a popular model for potential recruits to the SE ROCU. There were certain built-in safeguards for police officers to be able to return to their original force at any time, but there were no guarantees as to what post they would return to.

Up until this point in time, Sussex Police had been the lead force and officers were seconded to the SE ROCU. Sussex merely administered our processes linked to HR and Finance as well as offering some operational support in relation to the completion of authorities required under RIPA (Regulation of Investigatory Powers Act), aligned to investigations etc. This suited most people better and Sussex had a very clear understanding of their role in all of this.

Thames Valley, on the other hand, viewed things differently and operated in a way that suggested we were 'owned' by them when this was not the case. Sadly, we were lacking our own identity and branding to some extent and this was exacerbated by the fact that we did not have our own policies and processes. We had always relied on Sussex Police to lead us in these respects. This clearly left the Unit vulnerable and no single force's policies are designed to deal with the uniqueness of a regional entity. We had to operate day to day across a number of force and even regional boundaries. Many of Thames Valley's policies were insufficiently flexible to cater for this and therefore it was a little like trying to force a round peg into a square hole.

Additionally, it has to be said that, in my opinion and that of many others, Thames Valley's ways of working are decidedly archaic, in terms of the levels of bureaucracy imposed. Metaphorically speaking, it often appeared that there was a form to complete in order to complete a separate form in an effort to get things done! At times it was tedious in the extreme and led to considerable frustration on the part of those of us just trying to get the job done. We were often expected to attend training sessions or meetings and conferences, the content of which were specific to those officers and staff working for Thames Valley Police. The PDR or Professional Development Review was extremely cumbersome in terms of what individuals and their supervisors and managers were expected to complete. There did not seem to be any sort of common-sense applied to train ticket purchases or hotel bookings. These were always done through booking companies under so called 'procurement' rules who, of course, charged a percentage. This increased the cost of absolutely everything.

The levels of risk aversity were similarly ridiculous. Under the law, police vehicles do not need an MOT as they are regularly serviced to a high level. However, Thames Valley Police insisted on having MOTs carried out by local garages, incurring totally unnecessary expense. In addition to this, originally every month but later reduced to once a quarter, supervisors had to fill in a form relating to all police vehicles regarding a series of things. This included details of their tyre pressures and tyre tread levels as well as other information already in possession of vehicle workshops involving service and MOT dates. These requirements were all massively time-consuming and totally unnecessary. When I questioned why these particular requests were made, I was told that it was to lessen the likelihood of civil action being pursued by the drivers of police vehicles in the event of accidents! It begs the question as to how many times this had actually happened in the past in order to justify bringing about such processes. As far as I could work out, things such as this were unique to Thames Valley.

Around the time that we were first aligned to Thames Valley Police, we had another new Unit Head start with us. It always seems in policing that, as soon as a new individual is appointed to a key position, then this invariably leads to mass changes. Rather than taking the time to see how things are operating and what needs adapting, we nowadays seem to suffer from those who wish to make their mark at the earliest opportunity. This causes considerable and unnecessary chaos and uncertainty which then tends to negatively impact on performance. This was our third change of Unit Head in the space of five years, therefore hardly conducive to continuity and stability!

In terms of myself, in addition to my existing role, I was to take on the lead for Regional Prison Intelligence. Ultimately, my RIU manager's role would go, as the business of that Unit would integrate and merge with the newly formed Confidential Unit. The purpose of the regional prison intelligence function was to identify those individuals who continued to pose the most significant threat criminally whilst in prison. Many of the top tier of criminals continue to run their criminal enterprises whilst serving a term of imprisonment. The aim of the prison intelligence function therefore was to develop intelligence packages relating to those individuals and their criminal activities, with a view to then targeting them through an investigation. This serves two purposes. Firstly, it will hopefully disrupt their activities. Secondly, it may result in them being convicted of further offences and as a result, attracting an additional term of imprisonment.

# Kevin Moore

The problems experienced by the ROCU through its alignment with Thames Valley Police were to be further added to as a result of our involvement with what was known as the Priority Based Budgeting process. To this day, I am still not clear as to how or why, as a separate regional entity, we became embroiled in what transpired to be a hideous and destructive process. The experience was a wholly negative one and caused considerable damage and required some later retrospective action to put right some of the wrongs done. This, embarrassingly, included reinstalling things that had been removed. Unfortunately, as mentioned previously, with many things that happen in the public sector generally and the police service in particular, accountability for such errors appears to go totally unpunished. The PBB was never a requirement for the ROCU other than in the heads of some individuals, taking into account that it was in the process of growing its capability rather than cutting it. Whilst some savings were necessary as ROCU budgets had been cut slightly by the Home Office in line with central government policy linked to austerity, this did not, in my view, require a wholesale root and branch approach.

The outcome was that certain operational elements of the ROCU were either dispensed with in their entirety, such as my highly productive intelligence development team, or were cut to such levels that inevitably their ability to function was impaired. Not unusually, I was to find myself at the forefront of some difficult situations. This involved the redeployment of some of my staff, as well as matters regarding my strongly-held views relating to the direction of travel for the SE ROCU more generally. Once again, I seemed to be viewed as the problem, rather than the potential solution. In terms of the redeployment of staff, I was keen to ensure that fairness prevailed and that regulations in terms of police officers, and force policy in terms of police staff, were complied with. This put me at odds with senior management who appeared to think that they could operate outside these in order to achieve what they wished to put in place for the future. This included requesting the assistance of the Thames Valley Police Federation. Whilst I have no firm evidence to back up what I am saying, I have little doubt that my name was regularly blackened behind closed doors during an array of meetings. I similarly have no doubt that the impact of my approach to these issues ultimately 'did for me' as I was seen as a troublemaker. However, more of that later.

I wish to finish this section on a positive note. Despite all the problems that the ROCUs generally and the SE ROCU specifically have faced, the concept is sound. Law enforcement does most definitely need a regional response effectively linking together the local and national. In terms of results, there have been many positive outcomes both within the SE Region as well as elsewhere as regards investigations undertaken. These have been achieved as a result of the hard work, dedication and professionalism of those officers and staff involved. Often, they have had to do this in the face of unnecessary resistance from both inside and outside the police service. The former is to my mind inexcusable, the latter slightly more acceptable. What I mean by this is that individual forces and their chief officers as well as other senior ranks have, in my opinion, been guilty of looking at developments regionally as a negative thing rather than a positive event. Too often, these views have been short-sighted. They have been seen from a standpoint that further development regionally will impact on police force budgets and resources rather that considering what is best for law enforcement U.K. This could, I suppose, be equated with the analogy of 'turkeys voting for Christmas'. This is because that in order to provide a better response to serious and organised crime investigation, then perhaps some of the existing resources channelled into this activity at a force level would be more effective if utilised at the regional level. Therefore, some chief officers and other senior leaders within forces view this only as a reduction of their resources rather than seeing it as operating for the greater good.

Suspicion outside the police service itself is perhaps easier to explain. Police and Crime Commissioners (PCCs) are to a large extent focused on delivery of policing at the local level. Therefore, they may inevitably see the migration of resources from the force level to the regional one as a negative event. Politicians at local as well as national level may also inwardly have similar concerns. Whilst this should not be used as an excuse, it does perhaps assist understanding. What I don't get and refuse to accept is the lack of strategic vision demonstrated by some chief officers and other senior ranks. These are the very people who are supposed to display such abilities when considering what is best for the police service and law enforcement more generally. Those that have chosen to display ambivalence to the issue or at worst open hostility, need to take a good look at themselves. They need to attempt to see what can be achieved for the all-round benefit of law enforcement generally rather than how it may impact on their individual areas of responsibility. Too much effort has had to be expended over the past few years in trying to justify to the unbelieving that which clearly needs to be addressed. This has served only to dull the energy and enthusiasm of those tasked with delivering a future working model. We all need to get behind the concept and do our utmost to deliver something which will be sustainable for many years to come.

# CHAPTER 8 – LOOKING BACK

❖ Back to the future? Reinvention of the wheel? Just how many ideas are really new ones? eg neighbourhood policing.

❖ Is policing really that complex? What, why and who has made policing so difficult?

❖ The future? – should we draw on the past in order to consider the future?

❖ Do the public really understand what they want or do the police know best? The changing relationship between the police and the public.

❖ The impact of austerity.

❖ Dinosaur or forward thinking and what is 'Old School'? – towards the end.

❖ Looking back – 'constructively belligerent', 'enigma'?

❖ The best years of policing?

❖ Political correctness and its impact on policing – an insider's view.

If I were to write my own career epilogue and try to show what I wanted to achieve, then I like to think the following might be appropriate, taking into account what others have said about me. I hope the reader doesn't feel I appear conceited - I am far from perfect and have acknowledged my shortcomings and mistakes in this book. Whilst thankfully I am still alive and able to tell my story, many of us do at times reflect on our lives and careers in an attempt to gain some insight into how others may have seen them.

In writing *My Way*, I have attempted to show the reader, and in particular those who don't know me, that throughout my career, I always tried to do the right thing. This may not have been to the liking of others, but more important to me was the fact that I always attempted to be true to myself.

This was, at all times, more important to me than doing things which may possibly have shown me in a better light. The readers of this book will hopefully be able to draw those conclusions for themselves. If not, then I have failed to achieve one of my initial objectives when I set out to write this book. Some may ask themselves why this is so important to me? The reason is simple. I wanted to be able to show that despite the changes that have taken place in policing over the years, there is still hopefully room for individuals who wish to serve the public and support their colleagues in the best way they can. I have never deliberately set out to treat any individual unfairly, whether they be a member of the public or somebody who may have a criminal background, or indeed an individual who is a part of the same organisation in which I have worked.

Nothing I did was done for personal glory, but because it was my responsibility and duty. I never lacked ambition but by the same token I do not believe I was ever driven by it. For me, it was always about doing my job to the best of my ability. It was important for me not to be found wanting, and never to shirk the responsibilities that went with a leadership position. I tried to face every crisis with a determination to overcome the most difficult things that policing could throw at me. I believe that I possessed an inbuilt wish to serve and protect the public as defined within the role of Constable. I like to think I never put my own interests first and in this respect that I was selfless, sometimes to my own detriment when standing up for others. I certainly aspired to demonstrate the very best in terms of what is expected of a police officer. Finally and I suppose selfishly, I hope that at least some will remember me for what I achieved and for what I stood for in terms of some form of legacy.

I have enjoyed the experience of recalling some memories, both good and bad, that have been responsible for ultimately assisting in developing me into the person that I am. There is one thing for certain. As in any walk of life, policing will continue to develop. Policing has given me a life that is unique in nature. I have seen and experienced things that the vast majority of the public will never encounter. I have also had the privilege of working with some of the finest men and women possible. Without them and their support, it would not have been possible for me to personally achieve all that I have, or indeed we have, together. Therefore, I owe them a tremendous debt of gratitude.

I firmly believe that I, and those working with me during the same period of time, experienced the very best years of policing. The job itself was great, I worked with a fantastic group of people, the money was reasonable and there was the opportunity to have a bit of a laugh in down times, often in the face of adversity. I would like to think that officers of the future will experience something similar, although I very much doubt that those experiences will be as positive as that of mine or my colleagues. I say this as a result of having spoken to those currently serving and are at the early or middle stages of their careers. One thing is certain, however. We will never be able to turn back the clock in order to get those times back!

So, what have I made of it all when it comes to looking back? Is policing better now than it was previously, as many current senior leaders attempt to tell us all? Is it a case of back to the future and nothing more than a reinvention of the wheel? Is neighbourhood policing for example, a new concept or has it always been there?

The description of what policing should look like, at the point of its inception as laid down by Sir Robert Peel, is arguably pretty much the same as today. Is policing that complex therefore? I firmly believe that the concept of policing is fairly fundamental. Over the years, however, commentators, and in particular, academics, have been fascinated with the issues involved in policing. Many of these people, together with senior police officers, past and present, have often appeared to over-analyse what is required in terms of policing provision. After all, only a certain number of ideas are available in terms of the development of a policing model.

The Home Secretary, Government Ministers and Senior Police Officers have often waxed lyrical in recent times about Neighbourhood Policing. This is not new. It is what policing has always worked towards achieving. My generation of police officers, and the many before, all grew up with beat policing and its various iterations. What is that if not Neighbourhood Policing? My father spent six years as a village bobby. What is that if not Neighbourhood Policing? No, I am sorry, but the reality is that there is nothing new these days in policing, save for the development of new technology. Once all of those involved with the future development of policing understand this, then perhaps we can get down to the serious business of deciding how we go about achieving what it is that the public wants, rather than constantly tinkering around the edges.

This therefore once again begs the question: 'Do the public know what it is that they really want from policing?' I believe that they do but the simple fact is that they want too much, compared to what the Government is prepared to pay for or indeed what the public are willing to pay, bearing in mind policing is financed through taxation, both centrally as well as locally. The simple fact is that the public expect an emergency response, neighbourhood policing and real visibility, and they expect the police to be able to police the road network and also to investigate and detect crime. We cannot any longer expect to deal with everything that fits into these broad categories and therefore choices need to be made. The time is well overdue, in my opinion, for a Royal Commission to be undertaken on policing in this country. The last one took place in 1960 and therefore another one needs to happen as soon as possible. Whilst, for many years now, successive governments have resisted calls for one, we cannot, in my view, justifiably ignore the need for one. Such a development would assist what I believe to be the existing dichotomy with policing where, on the face of it, society wishes to enjoy a fairly liberal approach to the way that they live their lives. At the same time and underneath this, they also appear, at least on the face of things, to want the police to be tough in terms of the way in which they carry out their responsibilities. We therefore need to decide once and for all what it is that we want from our police service.

The problem of austerity has clearly had a major effect on policing. Whatever spin individuals attempt to put on the situation, as previously mentioned, smaller cannot be better under any circumstances when it involves public sector service provision. I have become bored and tired with the platitudes used by some of today's generation of chief police officers. They have often used statements to the effect that the challenge of reduction in police budgets may, somewhat perversely in my opinion, be viewed as a positive opportunity, because their policing model is able to deal with the situation as presented. What arrant nonsense! How can a force such as Sussex reduce its numbers from around 3200 to approximately 2500 and expect to perform at levels previously achieved? It is frankly ludicrous but that is the reality of the situation. The figures rarely, if ever, get a mention either by chief officers or indeed, PCCs.

The problem is that it will take radical change at central government level, not to mention considerable funding, to even get back to the numbers that previously existed. I have been asking myself constantly, 'Where is the leadership at

NPCC (National Police Chiefs Council) level prepared to take the fight to the Government?' We have seen this happen recently within the NHS and I would therefore expect to see similar from police leaders. They need to forget about their personal aspirations for their knighthoods or equivalent and get on and do the right thing! This is not a time for shrinking violets but for characters such as Mike Barton, the former Chief Constable of Durham Constabulary. He was prepared to be controversial where necessary in order to advance the needs of policing and, dare I say it, he was a real character. There now appear to be too many clones.

Is policing better now than previously? Of course, such a question is entirely subjective. What is definitely true is that what we have now is very different to what existed previously. What I would also contend is that the pace of change has been greater recently than it ever was previously. Technology has had a major part to play in this. When I first joined, the most technical thing in existence was the police radio system. Messaging between forces was undertaken through the use of a teleprinter, and electric typewriters were a relatively new development. The concepts of what made up policing were also an awful lot different when I joined. There was in those days basically uniform patrol, CID and the traffic department. Officers still 'walked beats' and certainly in Brighton, on occasions, we made 'points' with our Sergeants when they would sign our pocket books to that effect and woe betide you if your pocket book was not up to date at the time! Discipline was much more in evidence in those times than ever it is nowadays. In fact, arguably, it barely exists now and those of us who aspired to continue to practice its virtues, ran the risk of being at best referred to as 'old school' and at worst, a 'dinosaur'.

Therefore, what are the most obvious changes to policing over the years? Accountability is far greater now than ever it was previously. Elements of this must of course be very good for society and it is right and proper that any public-sector organisation, such as the police service, is accountable to the public that it serves. However, the downside of some of this accountability is that it has induced a fear in police officers, both at the front end as well as at senior levels. There is now an in-built fear of doing something wrong and therefore this has often led to inertia in recent times and a reluctance to make decisions, in my opinion. Stalling of decision-making is a problem, both in terms of longer-term strategic development and, of course, is potentially catastrophic in relation to operational decision-making. Operational commanders may 'freeze' at a critical point if they become excessively concerned with the outcome of their decisions. This may have serious and possibly fatal consequences in certain circumstances, such as police firearms-led operations.

Clearly, a balance needs to be achieved and there have been far too many instances where police officers at all levels have been subjected to ridiculously long investigations of either a criminal or misconduct nature or indeed both. I have covered some of this previously in relation to what is now the IOPC. This in-built fear cannot be good for any organisation, especially one such as the police. In my opinion therefore, there needs to be a radical rethink as to how we want the police service to operate in the future. This is a priority because, at the moment, the police feel hamstrung. They are in effect damned if they do and damned if they don't and that position is totally unacceptable. We therefore need to ensure that we are careful about what we wish for. To use a phrase used in the past, 'Do we want a police force or a police service?' There is a difference in my view, and for the majority of my police service, I firmly believe that we were more of the former than the latter. In speaking to friends over the years who have never served as police officers but are law-abiding individuals who want to get on with their lives, I believe that the majority also wish to see a greater emphasis put on a stronger form of policing, in terms of enforcement. This goes back to previous comments that I have made where I have stated that I believe the vast majority of society do not put forward their views, but the vociferous minority do, and they are the ones who get heard. The majority of the general public, in my opinion, don't wish to know about the 'dirty' side of policing but want the organisation to get on with dealing with bad things and the bad people doing these.

An excellent example of where things have radically changed within the police as well as other organisations such as the military, involves the development of what is commonly referred to as the issue of 'political correctness'. I firmly believe that this issue has become the bane of all our lives in general terms. I also believe that it has had a detrimental effect on policing, as well as other areas of the public sector. There is an irony to this insofar as, quite rightly, there has always been a need to ensure fairness and equity, whether this be in the workplace or within society more generally. However, I believe that in attempting to achieve this at work, we have effectively created a monster that is now totally out of control.

This has served to create a very unhealthy environment where individuals are now scared witless to speak their minds for fear of what they say upsetting someone and thereby leading to allegations of racism, sexism or some other form of discriminatory behaviour. This is very sad indeed. It creates suspicion and at times, paranoia. I know that some officers and staff have openly told me on many occasions that they would never consider telling a joke in an open environment anymore, for fear of somebody present taking exception to what was said.

# MY WAY

In my early days at Brighton and Hove, I was chairing the Daily Management Meeting one morning. This was the forum where all Operational Commanders, normally inspectors and above, met to discuss the events of the past 24 hours and ensure that appropriate responses were in place to incidents that had occurred. Earlier that morning, I had received a phone call from one of our local MPs, complaining about a group of travellers who had set up camp on the Hollingbury Golf Course in Brighton. Under existing legislation, a police Superintendent can issue an order for such groups to be forced to leave if the location where they are based is deemed to be an 'inappropriate stopping place'. A golf course would fit the necessary criteria. Therefore, in the meeting, I said I would sign the necessary authority and that on the cross-over of shifts at three o'clock that afternoon, I wanted officers to attend the location and remove the traveller group. An Inspector present queried whether I felt that such action may be a little hasty and that perhaps we should be considering the welfare of the group, especially any children who might be present. I said that I wanted them moved. To emphasise the fact that I expected this to happen and without any further discussion, I said, 'I don't care if we have to mount machine gun turrets in order to deal with them, but I want them moved on!' Now obviously, the terminology used was used in jest, as I believe the vast majority of those present accepted. However, what I said was subsequently relayed to Paul Curtis who advised me to be careful because such comments could end up being shared by somebody with the *Argus* newspaper. Whilst I understood the point that he was making, what a sad situation where something such as this is taken out of context quite deliberately by a colleague, just to make a point.

In a practical sense, this drive for equality can also mean that organisationally, we are in danger of bringing in a form of positive discrimination through the back door. Whilst positive discrimination is still illegal, as indeed is affirmative action if this involves 'quotas', there are very real concerns that, in a covert manner, this is potentially the end result at least. Chief Officers, in particular, appear to be obsessed with ensuring visible increases in so-called under-represented groups ie females, black and minority ethnic as well as LGBT officers and staff. This can potentially upset the true balance which should be based solely on merit.

This environment has also created a situation whereby individuals have been given a totally unrealistic expectation of what is available to them in terms of career advancement. Additionally, in attempting to level up the playing field for women with child care responsibilities, we have, in my view, gone too far the other way. I feel that this is particularly the case with the police service. This, in some cases, has had a detrimental effect on performance and has bred resentment across the board. Interestingly and perhaps somewhat perversely, some of this resentment actually comes from women without children who see what is on offer as discriminatory to themselves. Therefore, I would argue that, far from achieving what it set out to achieve, in some cases it has served to cause problems unforeseen by those promoting such change.

I have witnessed at first hand over the years some quite ridiculous situations which have culminated in full-scale, time-consuming investigations which, whatever the outcome, ultimately benefit no one. Individuals have lost their jobs or have had their careers ruined, simply because some individuals are not prepared to act in an adult or common-sense manner. On the most appropriate of occasions, surely it is better to confront something or someone at the outset in order to prevent unnecessary escalation. That is not to say that, in the most serious of cases, proper and robust intervention should not take place.

In fact, the opposite is correct. However, where it gets to a point that managers and supervisors are fearful of taking action to deal with problematic staff or poor performance for fear of being the victim of a spurious complaint, then in my opinion the balance has gone too far the other way.

This is indeed something that happened to me. In what transpired to be my last year of service, I experienced this at first hand. I had not intended to retire at the point that I ultimately did. However, after what happened to me, I felt that I had no other alternative. I suppose I was guilty of being naïve enough to think that, with my background and experience, I was unlikely to become a victim of a wrongful allegation or allegations as regards my conduct towards those working for me. I had always enjoyed an excellent working relationship with those for whom I had a managerial responsibility. This had been supported by feedback received either directly or via others. I had always believed that I treated my staff fairly and without favouritism. I recall an individual reminding me at my retirement celebration of an analogy I had been heard to use when looking after my staff. I used an example of an engineering company. In order to get the best out of any company's machinery and equipment, it required a regime whereby regular servicing was provided. I viewed staff similarly. In any organisation reliant on individuals to get the job done, so to speak, then we needed to ensure that we looked after and supported our staff who were our main asset. I had always felt that I had indeed practiced what I had preached and that team building and managing and leading staff was one of my strongest suits.

Having assumed my new role as the Regional Prison Intelligence Manager, it was determined, in line with the national direction, that the two entities of counter-terrorist and serious and organised crime prison intelligence capabilities should be integrated. There was no issue with this as far as I was concerned. It made complete sense as Counter-Terrorism's approach to prison intelligence was very similar to our own regarding serious and organised crime. They were targeting those subjects who were involved in CT-related issues whilst they were in prison.

However, things had occurred involving issues with some of our staff, whilst we were still a part of the ROCU, that had never been properly resolved. Much of these related to our operating model which consisted of a small regional intelligence 'hub' with the main resourcing being based in force areas and owned by them. This inevitably caused tensions and additionally meant that there was a lack of clarity of purpose for this whole area of business. We were therefore always seemingly trying to 'invent' ourselves, and managing the expectations of staff within the hub was very difficult, which caused internal friction on occasions. These problems were therefore carried over, right up to the point where the integration of the two units was scheduled to take place in March 2017. These problems in the main were related to the relationship between the staff at the operational level and their first line manager who reported to myself. Whilst I had triggered an attempt at conciliation in August 2014, the situation was still ongoing in March 2015 and had led to the involvement of a senior business manager. Despite her suggesting it, the staff concerned refused to enter into a further conciliation attempt. Rather than the business manager ensuring that the staff involved either 'put up or shut up' at that point, the whole thing was never resolved and was therefore allowed to fester potentially. Whilst there is a huge amount of other detail which I do not intend to go into here, this history unfairly provided the bedrock to what was to take place subsequently and was used accordingly. This was despite the fact that this put those involved, including myself, in danger of being victims of double jeopardy. This simple fact was ignored, however.

The culmination of this was that the new SE CTU line management decided that a 'cultural audit' would take place which was a term and a process that nobody, least of all me, had ever heard of, let alone experienced. Basically, its aim was to attempt to glean from staff within the team their views and opinions as to how the Unit was run and to identify any issues and problems. The object, as I was informed, was to then put measures in place in order to rectify these to the benefit of all, including the organisation. However, what actually took place, in my opinion, was a trawl for so-called evidence to then subsequently justify a full-scale investigation against the first line supervisor and myself. We were served papers alleging gross misconduct on 22nd May 2017 and were both placed on other duties. There then ensued what can only be described as a very protracted and long-winded investigation which, it has to be said, appeared to be heavily weighted in favour of the complainants. The interpretation of 'balance of probabilities' in terms of the evidential burden appeared to me to have a detrimental effect on any explanation provided by me, as well as any evidence that I submitted to the investigation. The allegations themselves, in summary, amounted to oppressive conduct or potentially even bullying, if believed. This was something that I had never been accused of in the whole of my previous service. Yes, I admit that I have always had a robust and direct approach to leadership and management. However, to me, bullying equates to a concerted and determined course of action against an individual or group of people, in an effort to undermine them and with the potential aim of getting them to move on ultimately.

The instances specifically referred to were, in some cases, actually quite ridiculous and without foundation, and worse still, some which I could actually prove to be false. However, this seemed to be ignored by investigators and decision-makers alike. In addition, the timing of the investigation was, in my view, highly significant. If all the events referred to occurred when the Regional Prison Intelligence Unit was a part of the SE ROCU, why was it that the investigation was triggered at the point where the line management moved over to the SE CTU? Unfortunately, I do not currently have the evidence to support what I believe to be the case, only suspicion. However, I feel that the origins for the investigation against myself, potentially at least, are founded in my differences of opinion with previous senior managers, some of whom were well-known to one another. I have no doubt whatsoever that certain conversations took place regarding me and the perceived difficulty that I presented, and therefore my card was marked as a result. The investigation undertaken would then serve the purpose of killing two birds with one stone.

However, those involved probably underestimated me in terms of the lengths that I was prepared to go to, in an effort to defend myself. Also, I was able to supply a considerable amount of character testimony from staff who had recently worked for me which showed me in a positive light. Additionally, this completely contradicted the so-called evidence against me. However, despite all of this and after more than eight months, I was to receive 'management advice'. This is the lowest form of outcome from such an investigation, other than exoneration which I was never naïve enough to believe would happen! Indeed, it is not even considered to be a sanction as such. Therefore, in the circumstances, it transpired to be the best outcome that I could realistically have expected. My main question therefore is simply this. How did something that started off as allegations involving gross misconduct which, if proven, is job threatening, become 'management advice'? The administration of this advice told me all that I really needed to know. Having very belatedly received written details on what it was that I was to receive advice about, I had prepared a written response. This, I circulated to those who were to give me the management advice. At the meeting, when I attempted to give my explanations to each matter raised, I was immediately told that my response demonstrated why it was that I needed to receive the advice. Apparently, I was expected to show contrition and regret for what had occurred, even though management advice is not a sanction. In addition, I still did not believe that I had actually done anything wrong. From my point of view, there was no reason whatsoever for me to be contrite. The fact that I still disputed everything levelled against me was not considered to be appropriate and therefore my explanations were deemed to be totally irrelevant. I was and still am angry with the response that I received. There was absolutely no objectivity shown whatsoever by those involved. As far as they were concerned, it appeared to me that the allegations had been made and because they were made by more than one person, then they must be correct. This was still the case, even though I could prove that a number of issues raised were completely false. Evidence did not seem to form any part of the equation!

My main concern is that it seems that if individuals don't like the approach of their supervisors and managers, then they can complain, alleging whatever they like, and if a number of individuals jointly complain, then they will be believed whatever. If this is the case, this stance has grave implications for those holding positions of responsibility. I was, in my own mind, guilty of nothing more than trying to get a group of individuals to do their jobs. I was prepared to challenge, as I always have done, issues relating to poor performance or excessive periods of sick leave or other forms of paid absences. I was also prepared to challenge resistance amongst certain staff members who seemed to feel that it was appropriate to fail to follow reasonable and lawful instructions. Frankly, this outcome only served to support my view that sadly the police service has lost its way in terms of management and leadership. We are now in real danger of allowing the 'tail to wag the dog'.

I had a female member of staff who worked part-time with her hours spread over three days. I was concerned how often she appeared to be away from work. So I requested a breakdown over a ten-month period of her allocated work hours and then how many hours of annual leave, sick leave, dependents leave and parental leave that she had taken during that time. I was horrified to be informed that she had actually been absent in excess of 25% of the total allocated working time. When I raised this with the HR team, I was told that she was operating in accordance with the policy, even if not within the spirit in which it was intended. Therefore, no formal action resulted. I addressed this directly with the member of staff concerned in an effort to get her to understand the impact of what she had been doing. This individual attempted to use this against me when the complaints were made leading to the investigation previously referred to. When I attempted to justify my stance on this matter as part of my response to the investigation, it was questioned as to why I had addressed the matter, rather than the first line manager! What on earth had that got to do with anything?! The fact was that the matter needed tackling but sadly, other than myself, nobody else seemed the slightest bit bothered or interested!

I had made up my mind, within three days of being served papers alleging gross misconduct, that whatever the outcome of the investigation, I was going to retire. I had simply had enough and was tired of all of the political infighting and the way in which things were going generally.

# MY WAY

I honestly believe that I have been a victim of some form of constructive dismissal. The sad thing is, that around eighteen months previously, my first line manager had advised me that I should start to take a back seat and relax. He suggested that I had more than done my bit and I should just confine myself to doing the basics that my job required of me and just continue to draw my salary. What a sad indictment on the way things have progressed in the police service if this is the attitude of those now employed within senior positions. Sadly, however, my drive and determination to continue to try to do my level best to develop the organisation had appeared to have backfired on me. Anybody who knows me will straightaway say that doing as little as possible is simply just not me. Therefore, I took the view that enough was enough and that my time was coming to an end, one way or another. I owed it to my wife Ann, my family and to myself to go. I had wanted to work sufficiently long enough to pay off my mortgage and may even have continued to work until state pension age, but I simply could not face the prospect. I would rather pay off my mortgage with savings available and disappear off into the sunset and enjoy my retirement. To quote the singer Johnny Nash, 'I could (sic) see clearly now'. So, on 1st August 2017, I gave notice of my intention to retire from the date of my 61st birthday in January 2018. For the last period of my service following the service of papers upon me, I was working directly for the most recently-appointed Head of the SE ROCU. She is an individual, I am pleased to be able to say, I respected and she in turn respected me. I undertook a number of pieces of useful work for her which were always well received and appreciated. Therefore, at no time did I feel side-lined by her. In fact, quite the contrary.

Therefore, I am left to pose the following question to myself and to the reader, 'Am I a dinosaur, old school, an enigma and/or constructively belligerent?' In my opinion, I am probably a little of each if I am honest, but I chose to view the terms in a positive sense. If the question is, 'Do I believe in some of the old-fashioned values and beliefs?', the answer is, 'Yes'. 'Do I believe in standing up for what I believe is right and in so doing attempt to display moral courage, even if it might be to my own detriment?' Then the answer is an unequivocal, 'Yes'. 'Am I prepared to challenge what I believe to be poor performance or behaviour?' The answer is once again, 'Yes'. These answers will inevitably mean that all the above descriptions which have been used to describe me in the past have been both relevant and accurate at different times. If this has meant that some have found me difficult to manage, then I accept this. However, this does not mean that I am wrong or that my approach should be perceived as difficult or destructive. I have always believed that this is a fundamental part of my job.

What it does mean is that my time has come and gone. I believe that my type is no longer wanted within the police service. Sadly, in my opinion, we appear to have reached a point where we are prepared to accept second best or worse, because organisationally we no longer have the stomach or desire to demonstrate robust leadership and management styles. It is unlikely therefore that we will ever witness what I refer to as the good times ever again.

Nowadays sadly, self-preservation seems to be the name of the game. Organisationally, the police service can no longer boast the characters and potential mavericks that arguably used to appear to thrive in policing. This is sad in my opinion and it is a view that is held by many.

Why is this so? Perhaps it is more to do with a reflection of society as a whole rather than being specific to the police service. If we choose to look at party politics for example, where are the characters and 'big hitters' that used to previously hold power? I am thinking in this regard of the likes of Winston Churchill, Margaret Thatcher, Edward Heath and Harold Wilson. They all had a massive presence about them and were respected even if they were not necessarily liked.

In my opinion, the police service no longer contains risk takers but rather individuals and so-called leaders who are fairly non – descript, bare no uniqueness and appear to be clones. This has in turn led to a group of senior leaders who do not appear to possess a voice as such either singularly or jointly. There is what I see as an almost visible weakness not the power and standing that appeared to exist in years gone by. I have real difficulty now in remembering who the Chief Constables of the various forces are now whereas previously I seemed to know the vast majority of them.

I recognise that there are some who will be prepared to argue that what I am trying to describe has always existed to a greater of lesser extent. Even when I joined there were the old sweat PCs in existence who were always prepared to state that, 'The Job is fucked'. However, what was often relayed in jest in those days is sincerely meant in current times. Many individuals joining the police service now see it only as a short-term rather than a long-term career. That was never the case in years gone by. Many are now quite prepared to 'give it a go' but if it does not work out then they will leave without any hesitation. There are of course many and varied reasons for this situation to prevail as previously highlighted. However, I have never witnessed a situation like the current one in nearly forty years of policing. Morale is undoubtedly at an all time low especially within the more junior ranks. The police service is crying out for real leadership and real heroes. However, I wonder where they are going to come from in all honesty.

Did I leave the service bitter and twisted? The answer is a

definite 'No'. I have had a great time for the most part. I have been involved in things that many individuals only ever read about in books or see on the television. I feel privileged to have worked in an organisation with some of the best people ever to have been put on this earth in the form of most police officers. I can honestly say, hand on heart, that I did my best to make society a better place. I now look forward to a new chapter in my life in terms of my retirement. I feel that Ann and I have earned this. Ann has been with me right throughout my journey. I would not have managed it without her support. I believe that I pretty much achieved my full potential although I often wonder to myself what the ACPO ranks would have made of me! Most of all though I am pleased to be able to say that, 'I did it my way!'

# MY WAY

## APPENDIX A

*Daily Mail* (London)
April 9, 1993, Friday

BLACK WIDOW WHO WED WITH MURDER ON HER MIND: Gullible old ladies were easy prey, but this woman was to prove more than a match for the charmer from the bank
By: Paul Henderson

HOLDING hands under the Gretna Green sign, this handsome couple have an aura of mature romance, mutual trust in a shared future.

The camera lied. Though the ink was still wet on the marriage register as Jean Daddow smiled up at her bridegroom, charming but dishonest bank executive Terry Daddow, she had already begun exploring ways of having him murdered.

But that isn't the half of this murder case with a storyline that could have been lifted from a TV melodrama. You know the sort of thing - charming conman falls for femme fatale who turns out to be even more crooked. She not only uses underworld contacts to find a hitman but manages to get an innocent bystander framed for the eventual killing.

The plot took its final twist yesterday, when Daddow and her son Roger Blackman were convicted of conspiracy to murder. Hitman Robert Bell, a former soldier, was found guilty of murder and conspiracy.

At Hove Crown Court, Mr Justice Hidden remanded all three in custody for three weeks for reports and warned them they faced very long fixed-term prison sentences or life imprisonment.

The story of the rise and fall of the Daddows is set in the sleek and pretty town of Tenterden, Kent, a larger version of

# Kevin Moore

Miss Marple's arena, St Mary Mead.

By one of those crashing ironies, Tenterden is 'Britain's most honest town' - it made headlines recently when somebody left £700 behind in a shop and recovered the cash intact. Then a pensioner dropped £100 in the street and all but a wind-blown fiver was returned.

Thrice-married Terry Daddow and divorcee Jean Blackman were jokers in that Happy Families pack. Daddow, the banker, master of hard-luck stories, was talking elderly, often confused women out of money. His wife, the banker's former mistress, came to perceive him as a golden goose to be plucked, then slaughtered.

Start with Terry Daddow, assistant manager of Lloyds at Tenterden, an investment advice specialist. Old ladies really took to that nice Mr Daddow. He'd come to tea at their splendid houses, where they felt so lonely, and open his heart.

Tales of his failing marriage and the way he would miss his three sons, Justin, Elton and Oliver, could loosen purse as well as heart strings. At least one widow gave him £1,000 for a holiday in Austria, to ease his pain.

'Has the ability to quickly develop close rapport with colleagues and customers,' declared a management training course report on the assistant manager.

Aware of his knack, Daddow played with the idea of augmenting his £28,000 salary by parting lonely women from their money. Some were so unbusinesslike or generally confused that they'd never miss it; others were only too ready to give it away if asked right.

Take - as he did, to the cleaners - 81-year-old Clara Hooper, a childless widow. 'He had great charm - any woman would admit it,' she says. 'He always seemed to be suffering misfortunes and I felt sorry for him.'

The bank man offered to help with the gardening, and Mrs Hooper gave him a plot of his own, 'because he needed to feed five and that costs a lot'. Less, however, than it was to cost her.

Terry Daddow, thinking aloud, confessed to kind Mrs Hooper that her £240,000 home, where he visited three times a week, was the only place he could 'find real peace'. So she left it to him in her will.

Daddow appeared to be content with small pickings. Then he met a different calibre of female customer.

Mrs Jean Blackman called at Lloyds to sort out a problem over credit cards. She'd had a spell as a special constable, looking most dashing in the uniform, but events suggest that at heart she was more robber, or worse, than cop.

Jean, well past 40, remained attractive in a well-covered way. Fighting for her freedom at the trial, she took care to look matronly, hemlines far below the knee, discreet cosmetics and a crucifix flashing its subliminal message from her sombre frock.

However, staid, disapproving Tenterden onlookers remember her senior-bimbo image, 'a reputation for adulterous alliances' and her taste for mini-skirts up to here and cleavage displayed by necklines down to there, not to mention far too much blue eye-shadow.

But that was the reaction from gentlewomen of a certain age. Terry Daddow loved what he saw and became lodger at Rovael Cottage in Biddenden, with Jean and her unsuspecting husband, Alan.

As the affair escalated, the man from Lloyds made a literally fatal mistake: he bragged about the old ladies and the £250,000 house he'd been promised. Jean realised that he held the key to plunder in profusion and decided to marry him.

Whatever else, Jean Blackman - as she was then - cannot be accused of not looking ahead. Long before the wedding, she approached a drug dealer and asked if he knew of anyone who would murder Terry Daddow for, say, a thousand pounds.

The 23-year-old dealer, Roger Blackman, happened to be her son. Sure, Roger Blackman assured Mum, there'd be candidates.

Only then, each having divorced a partner whom they had been cheating, did Terry and Jean slip away to Gretna Green, where they wed on June 6, 1989. Biter bit, one of the most hackneyed plot developments in the whodunit arsenal.

He and Jean made a great team, and Terry Daddow's parasitic moonlighting flourished. Taking advantage of gullibility and old women's hunger for affection and conversation, they harvested perhaps £500,000.

Some of it came from 91-year-old Ann Burton and her family fortune from generations of wealthy sheep farmers. She fell for Daddow's sob-stories of a doomed marriage and the pain of missing his sons, who would live with his second wife, Teresa.

Mrs Burton, a retired Red Cross official, sympathised. After Daddow introduced her to his new wife, Jean, the widow paid for their expensive summer holiday and a Christmas break in a converted Kent oasthouse, providing extra seasonal cheer with a hamper of wine and food.

Just the starter, of course. Terry Daddow took to calling Mrs Burton 'Mum' and persuaded her that they had been close for 23 years, rather than the five years or so since she had met him. Ann Burton accepted the fantasy and called him 'Son'.

Cue for a Jean and Terry duet: their divorces had left them homeless, whatever were they to do? In the spring of 1990, Mrs Burton bought them Chapelfield in Northiam, East Sussex, £162,000-worth of mellow red hanging tiles, inglenooks and exposed beams.

Further gifts took the total milked from Mrs Burton to more than £200,000. The Daddows were kept busy, shuffling it between bank and building society accounts to cover their tracks.

Cover was needed, for by July 1991, Mrs Burton was complaining that her investment income had dwindled to a quarter of its previous figure. Apparently she made no connection with her 'son', but her nephew, 46-year-old self-employed mechanic Mike Pearson, started investigating Aunt Ann's astonishing largesse.

'Daddow would flatter her,' Mr Pearson explains, 'and at the same time, say things like, 'I don't know how I am going to pay my son's school fees'. He played on my aunt's generosity - and she was proud of her financial adviser. 'He's the man who looks after all my money,' she would say.'

The pair's approach to fleecing Clara Hooper, who'd bequeathed Daddow her house, was slightly different. Twice she gave him £3,000 to buy second-hand cars. There was a loan, never repaid, of £10,000 for 'legal costs' - the Daddows were fighting a builder's bill of £1,500 for work on Chapelfield.

Things were turning sour by the summer of 1991. Mrs Hooper, aware that Jean Daddow dominated her friendly bank man, grew a touch cooler. Learning that another patron had given them Chapelfield, she cancelled the bequest of her home.

Distressing, dangerous rumours were percolating through white-weather-boarded Tenterden.

Daddow's management course assessment had praised, besides his ability to charm and disarm, his grasp of the legal considerations of lending or borrowing money. Arguably, legal considerations were constantly on his mind, as the take increased.

Certainly he was suffering spells of acute anxiety and taking extended sick leave. In May, the assistant manager retired after 23 years with the bank. Jean still showed a confident front in Tenterden, but the gossip worried her husband.

And worry is too weak a word for what Daddow felt about the implications of an internal investigation by Lloyds. A bank spokesman confirms that a complaint had been made against him - the first in his long career. It came from Mrs Burton's relatives.

In the light of that, Daddow wanted to hand Chapelfield back to its donor and move to Scotland. Jean was having none of that, though.

She reminded son Roger of her query about a contract killer. He recruited a Walter Mitty character called Robert Bell, mainly on the grounds that 32-year-old Bell, from Headcorn, Kent, 'owed' him.

Bell was paid £7,000 to liquidate Mrs Daddow's husband. Inflationary, compared with the £1,000 she had envisaged during those heady days of courtship but, expecting to inherit £500,000, she considered it money well spent.

Initially, the hitman was a terrible disappointment to the would-be widow. He bought a crossbow and trailed the couple to Devon, where Daddow was to be polished off on holiday, but couldn't nerve himself to shoot.

Bell staked out Chapelfield and even got inside but then he went home again, no blood on his hands.

Yet Bell felt a sense of obligation and he had his pride. So he discarded the crossbow and, in November 1991, tried his luck with a shotgun. He knocked on Chapelfield's door and when Daddow opened it, Bell shot him in the chest at point-blank range.

Jean Daddow came downstairs to watch blood pouring from her husband's wound. She watched, or at least waited, for several minutes, needing to be sure that he was dead and that Bell was clear of the crime scene. Then she picked up the phone.

Another excruciating irony - the day Daddow died, the following personal column item appeared in the local paper:

# MY WAY

'DADDOW, Terry, Jean. Because of malicious gossip would like it known that they are happily married and together. Not guilty of fraud, theft or senility.' Bluff turned epitaph, it had cost the late Terry Daddow £14.56.

Now comes the final Christie flourish - a classic red herring sneered at by current queens of fictional crime. Real people, they sniff, simply don't behave like that. Only this time they behaved exactly like that.

Jean Daddow had conned the conman and hooked him, cold-bloodedly considered his despatch and brought about his murder. Now, in a manner of speaking, two more birds could be killed with one stone.

As his wife, standing to gain most from his violent death, she was prime suspect. And Mike Pearson, Mrs Burton's awkward, amateur detective nephew, had been making trouble. To any whodunit addict, Mrs Daddow's next move was inevitable.

Jean, the erstwhile special constable, pointed the finger at Mr Pearson. He had a grudge against her and her husband, she said, because they'd accepted his aunt's gift of the house where Daddow died. And Pearson was major benefactor under Mrs Burton's will, since both her husband and their son had been killed on active service during World War II.

In the early hours of November 27, 1991, Mike Pearson's three-bedroom house in Tenterden High Street was surrounded by armed police.

The phone started ringing at dawn, and when Mr Pearson's 15-year-old son Nicholas answered, he was ordered to secure the family Alsatian, then come out with his father and his 18-year-old brother Timothy - very carefully, hands above their heads.

Mike Pearson went off to interrogation. Jean Daddow did her best to stoke the fire under him by telling police that he was behind malicious slanders about her husband fleecing old folk.

But the frame fell apart the instant it was tested. Mr Pearson agreed that he had been unhappy about the money flowing from his aunt to the Daddows, and had shared his suspicions with the Fraud Squad at Canterbury. But there was the matter of a cast-iron alibi - he had been drinking in his local, the Vine at Tenterden, when Daddow was blasted. He and his boys walked free within an hour or two.

Mr Pearson, who is taking legal steps to recover £209,000 for his aunt, on the grounds that the Daddows exerted undue influence on her, argues: 'As far as Jean Daddow was concerned, I was going to be convicted of murder and sent to prison for a very long time. If she was convincing to the police, can you imagine the influence the Daddows had over old ladies?'

Clara Hooper, who gave the man from Lloyds so much, has launched a claim against his estate. 'He ingratiated himself,' she sighs, 'and I suppose it was a bit wet of me. He was a very skilled actor.'

So, as the Gretna wedding picture demonstrates, was Jean Daddow.

# MY WAY

## AUTHOR'S BIOGRAPHY

Kevin Moore joined Sussex Police at the age of twenty-one years in June 1978. His father was a serving officer with the Force at that time having joined in the 1950s. Sadly, his father died a few months after he himself had joined. This means that their joint careers span a total of over 60 years of policing.

After joining the police, the author spent his two-year probationary period at Brighton during which time he operated as a beat officer and area car driver/observer. Whilst there, he experienced a wide variety of policing situations as one would expect in terms of the cosmopolitan nature of a city the size of Brighton and Hove. Following this, he became a rural beat patrol officer at Camber near Rye in East Sussex.

A short while later, he entered the Criminal Investigation Department (CID), as a detective constable. This proved to be the beginning of a long and productive career as a detective during which time he climbed the ranks ultimately achieving the highest rank possible in the CID world of Detective Chief Superintendent when he was the Head of Sussex's CID. During his service he was the senior detective in charge of the CID at Hastings and Eastbourne. He also worked within the Professional Standards Department investigating complaints made against police officers.

He served as the Chief Superintendent and Divisional Commander of Brighton and Hove during which time he was responsible for all police operations in the City as well as working with key partner agencies including the City's Council. He took command of many large-scale public order demonstrations as well as other major public safety events.

During his detective career, he was a Senior Investigating Officer (SIO) with a responsibility for leading enquiries into homicide and other major crime investigations. He was viewed as being a highly competent senior detective. He was formerly a member of the International Homicide Investigators Association.

Following his retirement as a police officer in 2009 after more than thirty-one years of service, he took up a position with the newly formed SE Regional Organised Crime Unit as a civilian or member of police staff. This involved the role as the Regional Intelligence Manager and then subsequently that of the SE Regional Prison Intelligence Manager. This Unit has an overall responsibility for investigating the criminal activities of those involved in the commission of the most serious types of crime.

He fully retired from the police service in January of 2018.

He has been married to Ann for over forty years and has two grown up children and five grandchildren. He holds a BA (Hons) Degree in Public Sector and Police Studies and a Post Graduate Diploma in Police Studies. He is interested in football and cricket and is a season ticket holder with Brighton and Hove Albion FC and also now spends his time with his and his wife's Golden Retriever dogs and their four horses.

Printed in Great Britain
by Amazon